Disoriented

Disoriented

Embodied Life in Strange Times

※

AGNES R. HOWARD

CASCADE Books • Eugene, Oregon

DISORIENTED
Embodied Life in Strange Times

Copyright © 2026 Agnes R. Howard. All rights reserved. Except for brief quotations in critical publications or reviews, no part of this book may be reproduced in any manner without prior written permission from the publisher. Write: Permissions, Wipf and Stock Publishers, 199 W. 8th Ave., Suite 3, Eugene, OR 97401.

Cascade Books
An Imprint of Wipf and Stock Publishers
199 W. 8th Ave., Suite 3
Eugene, OR 97401

www.wipfandstock.com

PAPERBACK ISBN: 979-8-3852-3042-6
HARDCOVER ISBN: 979-8-3852-3043-3
EBOOK ISBN: 979-8-3852-3044-0

Cataloguing-in-Publication data:

Names: Howard, Agnes R., author.

Title: Disoriented : embodied life in strange times / Agnes R. Howard.

Description: Eugene, OR: Cascade Books, 2026 | Includes bibliographical references.

Identifiers: ISBN 979-8-3852-3042-6 (paperback) | ISBN 979-8-3852-3043-3 (hardcover) | ISBN 979-8-3852-3044-0 (ebook)

Subjects: LCSH: Quotidian; Everyday life. | US History. | Culture. | Civilization, Modern.

Classification: BJ1498 H89 2026 (print) | BJ1498 (ebook)

* Scripture quotations are from Revised Standard Version of the Bible, copyright © 1946, 1952, and 1971 National Council of the Churches of Christ in the United States of America. Used by permission. All rights reserved worldwide.

To Ellie, Hannah, and Ben, who have always known about Ohio

Contents

Acknowledgments ix

Introduction: Beautiful Ohio 1

Chapter 1: Good Things to Eat (Food) 11

Chapter 2: Continuing Education (School) 29

Chapter 3: Seeking Fortune (Work) 50

Chapter 4: Friends and Lovers (Marriage) 67

Chapter 5: Naked I Came (Birth) 89

Chapter 6: Never Done (Motherhood) 109

Chapter 7: Be Not Afraid (Faith) 128

Bibliography 153

Acknowledgments

A PROJECT SPANNING A period both long and personal opens many chances to appreciate the generosity of others. I am grateful to the editorial team at Cascade Books for their assistance and patience with this project. I am grateful to my family, my mother and siblings, and my husband, Tal, and our children. I am grateful to Jennifer Banks, Natalie Carnes, Bria Sandford, Anne Snyder, Ellen Koneck, Leah Libresco Sargeant, Amanda Ruud, Nadya Williams, Carrie Frederick Frost, Jillian Snyder, Alexandra Lembke, Laura Fabrycky, Meagan Saliashvili, and Elspeth Currie for rich conversations and for comments on some of this material. I am grateful to my colleagues at Christ College, the Honors College at Valparaiso University, for their good company and scholarship. I am grateful to students for ongoing conversations on these topics, and to Katherine Naylor for her work on this manuscript. I have received the high honor of thinking together on these topics with beloveds over years, and thank especially Christine Perrin, Suzie Park, Jill Karr, and Hilary Yancey for that. The debts and errors are mine. Thank you for bearing with.

Introduction: Beautiful Ohio

EITHER I'M CRAZY OR everybody else is, a friend of mine says at the start of most conversations. She is not primarily talking about politics. More often she names a part of life closer at hand. Confusions may come from the antics at somebody's wedding or what kids are learning in school or some new item in the grocery store. Confusion breeds disorientation, a sense of having misunderstood something fundamental and at the same time being misunderstood, so even honest effort to respect current manners fails to bridge distance between now and then, us and them. In parts of ordinary life, what an American adult might grow up to do and be, much has changed in the last century. Reassurances make things worse by misguided pretense of continuity, that the strange thing isn't really different: tastes like chicken! at least they're reading! that's how kids fall in love nowadays! Missteps in daily life—what to eat, how to parent, whom to trust—may stumble onto forks in the road with hard left-right choices, or may find no sound path at all, as though everyone is left to invent his own manners with all minefield in between. Disorientation is a reasonable reaction to this problem.

Feeling disoriented is reasonable. Recognizing what is strange about our own time and tracing how things got to be that way can help. The past sets conditions of life in the present, but not always intentionally. We live amid what others ahead of us chose, built, lost, celebrated, or wasted, plus the unpredictable consequences of doing those things. Time puts its stamp on us. What we pull forward with us into life—individually or corporately—puts our stamp on our times. Learning how to see one's own life as situated in time and stitching together facts with experience is a complicated project. It might also be a clear path out of disorientation when few seem available.

My grandmother can illustrate, by way of the state of Ohio.

Disoriented

My grandmother was not a sentimental woman. My mother took us to visit her often in summers in the 1970s and early 1980s when we were little, long drives with my siblings crammed unbuckled in the backseat. I regret that I knew my Baba mostly in her office as grandmother. Baba was miscast in a job description that, as far as I knew from the books I read, required grandmas to be sweet. Thus it was surprising ever to find her dipping into something like fancy. Sometimes, when narrating a memory from childhood, or being asked where in the world she would like to travel if she weren't living widowed in a brick house near Pittsburgh (besides dream destinations of the Holy Land or Czechoslovakia, the latter of which was impossible because it was then behind the Iron Curtain), she would break off and her voice took on an unusual singsong quality as she said, "Beautiful Ohio!" She pronounced it "beauty-full" Ohio.

That baffled me because I thought, A) What I had seen of Ohio was not beautiful, B) Ohio was basically a farm state with some defunct industry and the dirt and stink that went along with that in the mid-1970s, and C) if it were so beautiful, why did she stay in Pennsylvania? Even if Ohio were a great state—and I grew up in 1970s New York so I knew all about state greatness, state-as-empire, I heart NY—was *beautiful* the right word for a state?

My grandmother lived across the street from St. Mary's Roman Catholic parish in McKees Rocks, Pennsylvania, a neo-Gothic church built in 1905 to look like it belonged in a century and a country a long way away. The architect who designed it came from Ohio. Baba went to daily Mass there and to what seemed like nearly daily funerals. She played bingo in the church hall. Priests from St. Mary's came over occasionally to eat lunch at her table and she regaled them with the accomplishments of her sons, one a dentist and the other a lawyer. Only imagining my younger brother as the first American pope, a prospect that seemed entirely plausible for a time, made her prouder.

She liked having us visit, though that seemed clearest when we were about to drive back to upstate New York and she sat on the couch in the hallway watching us pack the car and told us that the house would be quiet after we left. She scolded us when we cried and hardly gave us opportunity to earn the epithet "lazy," one of her least favorite traits, since when we were at her house she kept us busy collecting yard waste, repairing roof tiles, carrying things up and down three flights of stairs to the attic, fetching canning jars from the cold cellar. We probably did look lazy, though, since

Introduction: Beautiful Ohio

there was not much else to do in her house. We planned our afternoons around flowers she had planted next to the house, four-o-clocks, which supposedly only opened at that time of day and which we tried to witness. Baba had two board games, Parcheesi and The Beatles Flip Your Wig Game. These she kept in a closet on the third floor in my aunt's old room and they were not worth the trip up. Meals at her house were regular: "twelve o'clock lunchtime," and dinner at five each night a few minutes after the rosary ended.

What I learned in school eventually allowed me to chalk up her singsong Ohio praise to nostalgia for a simpler way of life, golden days before dependency and decrepitude. My grandmother grew up on a farm. She and her husband and virtually everyone they knew, cousins, colleagues, compatriots, longed for the day they could move back to a farm. The men might end their lives still working in factories or mines or railroads but they never stopped hankering for the open field. My grandparents described the cousins who got to stay on the farm as the lucky ones. After history classes in college that taught about immigration patterns, industrialization, and assimilation, I thought I understood why they all felt that way about farms. My twenty-something college-educated idea was that finally I understood what my grandmother meant by Beautiful Ohio. I didn't have to agree that Ohio was beautiful, but I could place her longing, at least, recognizing what she was longing for and why. My education had served its purpose.

A few years ago though, when cleaning out sheet music from the piano bench in my mother's retirement-span house in Florida, I found pages from a song called "Beautiful Ohio." What could be the meaning of this? Did states have songs? (Yes.) Did popular-music marketers just before the 1920s think they could make money by selling songs specific to a state? (Yes.) Did other people think Ohio was beautiful, make a song about it, and did people know that song? They did. It occurred to me that the reason my grandmother sounded singsong saying "Beautiful Ohio" was that she was *actually singing a song*, at least that line of it.

What if, all along, she had been merely singing a song, not spilling out her own dreams or her private nostalgia, but absentmindedly mouthing a pop tune from her youth? Or maybe over time she adopted somebody else's lyrics to name her own different beautiful thing, that love of farm and family and goosefeather pillows, until it felt like "Beautiful Ohio" was her theme song, the way I felt like "We Are the Champions" had to have been written for when the Steelers won the Super Bowl in 1979.

Disoriented

"Beautiful Ohio" is a song from 1918. That would have been about the right time for my grandmother to hear it. She was newly arrived as a teenager in beautiful Ohio then, the state where she was born, where her family returned after a trip to the old country lasted much longer than planned because the First World War broke out around them. How excellent would that be, to have come over from abroad only to discover that the place where you landed was so universally admired that someone wrote a popular song about its beauty? In "Beautiful Ohio," a man sings about canoeing down the river, how he misses it and his beloved. But the phrase "Beautiful Ohio" doesn't belong to the songwriter. The adjective is built into the state's name. The French aristocrat Alexis de Tocqueville revels in this fact in his *Democracy in America*, the famous account he wrote of his trip to the United States, published about seventy years before my grandmother was born. The name of this great state comes from an Iroquois word meaning "Great River," embellished by the French explorer LaSalle into "Beautiful River." "Beautiful Ohio" is redundant, because the word "Ohio" itself names the beautiful, no additional adjective needed.

This is how Tocqueville praises the waterway in the nineteenth century: "The stream which the Indians had distinguished by the name of Ohio, or Beautiful river, waters one of the most magnificent valleys which has ever been made the abode of man. Undulating lands extend upon both shores of the Ohio, whose soil affords inexhaustible treasures to the laborer." He then notes that the river made a border between slave states and free states, Kentucky the land "which follows the numerous windings of the Ohio upon the left," and Ohio on the right bank. The air and the soil on both sides were the same. It was what people did that made a difference. Disapproval sharp, Tocqueville opines that on the left, "society seems to be asleep, man to be idle, and nature alone offers a scene of activity and of life." In contrast the right bank hosts a "confused hum" of industry, where "the elegance of the dwellings announces the taste and activity of the laborer; and man appears to be in the enjoyment of that wealth and contentment which are the reward of labor."[1]

Reward of labor was what drew my great-grandparents. The beautiful state, having moved from it the Indigenous people who named its river, was among the first new states in the new United States. The beautiful state explicitly excluded slavery in its founding and was early settled by people who sailed their wagons over from Massachusetts. It was later settled by people

---

1. Tocqueville, *Democracy in America*, 404–6.

Introduction: Beautiful Ohio

who sailed across an ocean so they could plow a field and grow a farm and make a life. My grandmother's parents did that. A magnificent valley, treasures from honest toil—that describes pretty well what my grandmother's family wanted from Ohio. Of course my grandmother thought Ohio was beautiful. She was made in Ohio and its promise of a good life brought her people there and kept pulling her memory back.

I have never lived in Ohio. I have no just claim to interpret Ohio. But I think about Ohio a lot. Ohio helps me think about other parts of life. Beautiful Ohio names the effort of finding your place in a history that you did not construct, and the chastened sense that others place themselves this way too, in ways very easy to misunderstand. Beautiful Ohio captions my snapshots of my grandmother's earthly paradise, of the reality I saw instead in its place, and of what I misunderstood about the inalienable things I was born to. My grandmother grew up in the morning of the twentieth century when the world was about to tip over. I could not enter her Ohio because what resettled in its place—strip malls and potholes and a river so polluted it caught on fire—looked unworthy of desire. One generation gets born into the leftover half-built, half-destroyed projects of the previous one, and finds that crossing the rubble may clear new streams or knock aside stones that block paths altogether. The generation born after the midpoint of last century walked into a place piled high with wreckage and lots of opportunity. With footing unsure, we tend to press too hard in some places or confuse remnant for ruin.

O beautiful Ohio, you are reminder of how difficult it is to know anything as it actually is, and why attempts to do so should not be reserved for philosophers. We can learn some things in theory and win a credential for learning them that we flash to gatekeepers who click a door open and nod us through, and then we feel proud and we *know* as for the first time. But knowing things in one way often makes it harder to know in another. Once in college I sat in on a single philosophy class and through the whole hour I had literally no idea what the teacher was talking about. I tried to understand, I really did, but even familiar words had turned obscure. Now and then a facet glinted in the light but only to warn me that thinking that way might ruin ordinary living. I fled the class and registered to be a history major. Later I went to graduate school to study history longer. Historical thinking is an accessible way for ordinary people to make sense of ordinary life. When I got a PhD after studying more history, my aunt and uncle bought me a roasting pan as a graduation gift and reported to my grandmother that she now had another granddaughter who was a doctor. To date, my grandmother had five. The daughters of my dentist uncle all had become dentists or physicians. Who, my grandmother asked, who else is a doctor? When they named me, my grandmother shook her head and said, "Nah! That's not a real doctor." And, besides, she said of me, who would ever read anything she writes, since her handwriting is like chicken scratch?

The writing of this book follows a beautiful stream between strange things to consider how embodied daily life has changed in an American lifetime. I follow its numerous windings through landscapes transformed by social norms. Looking downstream helps explain how things got to be the way they are. Looking upstream offers some clues for navigating strange times. Tocqueville justified his study trip in the United States on grounds that understanding problems inherent in democracy, the inevitable pattern of the future, could enable avoiding its worst parts and managing the good ones better. That is my intent in navigating some contemporary patterns.

My manner of navigating deserves explanation. I use two different kinds of writing to make a way through these topics. One reflects academic conventions about history, especially cultural and social history. I summarize broad changes and pay attention to events that signal change about how things are done, like going to school or planning a wedding. Unlike academic history taken strictly, these backstories are provided mostly to help explain the present. They are abbreviated, not exhaustive or much nuanced. They yield normative conclusions. The other kind of writing is autobiographical social history, illustrating some events from the view of my experience. It is not intended mostly as memoir. These personal portions engage the historical framing as a voice from within the period and as an angle of observation.

SETTING ONESELF INSIDE TIME

The way Americans do many things now is strange, but strange how? Strange according to what? It is hard to get far enough outside your own culture to size your culture up. To do so, being an outsider can be an advantage, like the advantage immigrants have. Those who come from another country have an angle for observation. But the past is a foreign country, as historians sometimes quip. Gazes backward do not look for a golden age. More often the project is finding something puzzling in the present and

Introduction: Beautiful Ohio

finding something else puzzling in the past, and then considering how one gave way to the other or what may be learned from the difference. History is a good tool, not a perfect one. Its revelations are partial. To help see parts of life in the present more clearly, I set them alongside historical frameworks, broad social and narrower personal ones. I observe, recollect, and send words back at things or events to make their shape visible, locating myself in the echoes of what happened, locating what happened in the outline of my life. For summaries of institutions like work or school, I follow timelines that belong with that topic. Next to those I place narratives in a timeline that starts with my grandmother.

This timeline starts with my grandmother because through my mother she was my embodied entry to American life. My grandmother did not start from nowhere and neither do these topics, so timelines sometimes reach further back. Her lifespan conveniently spans the twentieth century. The chapters move forward through that century somewhat chronologically and thematically, corresponding roughly with the order these experiences were supposed to occur, at least in my grandmother's day. We may finish school, start a job, make a vow, and have a baby, as points fixed on a timeline. Some things resist timeline sequence.

A little more autobiography can place me on the timeline started by my grandmother. My four grandparents were immigrants from Slovakia who settled in the industrial and mining areas of Pennsylvania and Ohio in ethnic Catholic enclaves. Their descendants took a course fairly typical to immigrant families in the twentieth century, parents working hard in farm or factory to give their children more education, the children becoming professionals and leaving traditional ways behind. Critics can fault the hypocrisy of American boasts about equality and prosperity, but in principle those ideals offered improvements, if not to all and not always in practice. Heroic deeds of those older people gave their children opportunity to do things they could not. Still, anyone whose life looks different from their parents' may know the feeling this brings: things are strange and you try to size them up but are rarely sure what is being asked of you. Obstacles removed in one place might block benefits in another or for different groups of people or strew mines into a separate sphere of life.

My parents moved to a university town in upstate New York and divorced. My mother raised us in New York and my father went back to Pennsylvania to teach chemistry at a small state college. Unlike my four siblings who, like my father, are good at math and science, I was a nerdy bookworm. Like my father, I got an advanced degree and have spent a couple decades teaching in small colleges. My life is not representative of how all things are for all Americans. But it has been lived under the scope of events and popular culture that set expectations for Americans in general in these decades.

My reactions to these decades may resonate with some readers more than others. My outlook on this time may sound typical of my generation, though I don't entirely identify with the generation assigned to me by birth. By the time generation-naming entered mainstream chatter, I was already grown into generic adulthood rather than tagged with X. Generational approaches bear insight but their judgments may be compromised or superficial, lumping and splitting in the wrong places. Those who were born near the middle of the last century might find the current world strange, but not only them. I argue that things actually are strange now, not only that they seem that way to me.

Narratives from my experience give examples of the practice of setting oneself inside history, allowing the facts of time and place to make one's life legible and vice versa. My grandmother handed down an interpretation, which I mistook, which history interpreted then for me more accurately and returned in shuffled layers of accuracy, mistake, and response, a combination that may turn out to be what I hand on, just as everybody else does for the artifacts of their time and place. Tacking back and forth between the world then and world now threads through realities gaped open by individualism and identity politics. Unlike current scripts for self-determination, this stitching denies that we make ourselves whatever we want to be. Our lives start as an event in somebody else's life, and we don't start from scratch. We had to go through some Ohio to get here.

The body connects each of us to others and to other fine and painful parts of creation. Our embodied life is shaped by freedom and finitude together, as theologian Gilbert Meilaender writes. The following chapters name experiences that do not lose value because our days are passing away. We are not just abstractions or loose spirits. We receive words in flesh. Christian belief has shaped my experience of embodied life, affirming that the material reality of our lives is given and good though subject to decay and expiration. Embodiment obligates some engagement in one's own time and place. I engage life in the United States from the vantage of this faith.[2]

---

2. Meilaender, *Bioethics*, 3–4.

Introduction: Beautiful Ohio

Personal experience placed alongside history allows not only telling what happened but how it feels. Tracing the development of things treated functionally as though they have no history, like soccer practice or dinner tables, shows us turning points or alternatives that might be retrieved. The very fact that things were done differently in the past can open eyes to present patterns taken for granted as normal or inevitable. One of the chief occupations of adulthood is recognizing as interesting or even lifesaving things that have been right there in front of your face all along.

PRESERVING WONDER FROM DISQUIET

Being finite creatures calls for examining particulars rather than abstractions. Therefore in the chapters that follow I attend to particulars, setting context first with brief historical sketch of the topic at hand, then offering narrative from family experience to illustrate how some things have gone strange. Next, I try to explain what went awry, what loose end unraveled or off-ramp got missed, before offering words on thinking better about some part of life. That echolocation seeks outlines of big shapes in daily life. Other topics worth sizing up escape these pages. Readers wishing that other categories had been studied, like communication or entertainment or travel or healthcare, imply support for my method and set their own fresh agenda for practicing it. By all means, readers can try this at home.

Chapter 1 centers on feeding the body. What is strange about food now is that plenty and convenience for Americans did not produce contentment but ballooned expectations and pulled food far from its sources and social context.

Chapter 2 moves to feeding the mind. What is strange about education now is that American kids may have fun in school, along with competition, inequality, and economic imperatives looming over classrooms. Technology that promised enrichment yielded distraction. Joy and wisdom are goods of education that some graduates may not reach despite many years in school.

Chapter 3 considers work. What is strange about work now is that Americans may build whole identities around work or its fruits without resolving its place in their communities, families, or the shape of their lives.

Chapter 4 turns to another human vocation, marriage. What is strange about marriage now is that more Americans can marry but marriage has become rarer and romance scarcer. By disaggregating components traditionally bundled in marital union, like love, commitment, permanence, and children, men and women are left lonelier.

Chapter 5 considers birth. What is strange about birth now is that healthcare and knowledge can make it easier, but to many women childbearing has come to seem too risky. Understanding pregnancy and birth better might build space to admire how humans come to be.

Chapter 6 regards motherhood. What is strange about motherhood now is that its job description grows ever more complicated and anxiety-producing no matter what moms do. Young adults contemplating parenthood are understandably ambivalent. Embodied care pays forward the gift each of us received in coming to life.

Chapter 7 wrestles with Christianity. What isn't strange about American Christianity now? Faith in my grandmother's day in my family meant a Roman Catholic parish, outside of which there was no salvation. In my mother's day, Pope John XXIII updated the whole Church. American Christians now, Catholic, Protestant, or Orthodox, may recognize kinship to each other but otherwise feel embattled or indifferent.

This book offers my attempt to make sense of changes specific to my time and place but relevant to readers who recognize how much has spun around them. Americans born before this century would have found spots in all my categories where new world-historical conditions overflowed with possibility, old obstacles swept away and abundant vistas ahead. Instead, choices and missteps closed up some possibilities and complicated others. That past helps explain a frustration common to this current decade among people who don't like how things are turning out and want to go back to the way things were before, when things supposedly used to be great. People might mean this literally. But the ache underneath also might be not for return to a perfect past, because actually there isn't one to make great again. I suspect it is more a wish to go back to the fork in the road or branching stream when opportunities were open, back to when, instead of being stuck with what happened, instead of having dumped garbage at the junction and taken a route that looked tempting, we could go back and clean up and take the other way. I may be reading the impulse too generously, that what is wanted in great-again sensibilities is a chance to redo things that the present shows we have screwed up. We screwed it up. It was what people did that made the difference. But maybe some generosity is warranted for the feeling that things are bad, the feeling that cries out for a corrective lest we miss beauty in the world and hope about what can be. Due wonder at the good of existence should not be choked by disquiet.

Chapter 1

Good Things to Eat (Food)

A COUSIN FROM SLOVAKIA came to the United States in the early twentieth century. While he was hungry, walking the streets, a man gave him a banana. He ate it to stop his growling stomach but wanted to spit it out. What kind of country was this, where people handed you food? What kind of country was this, where the food was so bad? The cousin found a job at the factory and got enough to eat. My grandmother liked to tell this story just to get to this part. One day the cousin went to the zoo and saw a monkey eating a banana. The monkey held the banana in one paw and stripped back the peel with the other before putting the fruit in his mouth. Oi! said the cousin, what kind of country is this? Even the monkeys here are smarter than I am!

America is a big country where most people were farmers until the late nineteenth century, when a lot of immigrants who also would love to have been farmers showed up to work in factories. Food cultures got diluted and scrambled when newcomers added theirs to the ones already present in the country. Technology rapidly changed what the country could eat and culture changed what we wanted to eat. The food choices we make are not always good, though we should know by now how to eat enough and eat well. Accommodating women's new roles away from home and kitchen, accommodating newly refined palates, accommodating the physical aspirations of the fit and affluent, American culture inflicted disorder on eating, misspending chances to raise standards of all through abundance.

A SHORT HISTORY OF AMERICAN FOOD: THE REVOLUTION

The short history of American food from the decade of my childhood starts with family dinner. In the 1970s, the housewife dinner was meat on a plate plus a starch and a vegetable. The prehistory of the 1970s dinner plate blends abundance and dislocation. In the late nineteenth century, railroads and refrigerated shipping made meat and warm-weather produce available year round. In the next century, canned and frozen foods and electric appliances transformed kitchens with modern conveniences for housewives. American food in the 1970s was subdivided by class, region, and season but was also homogenized. Those years dictated that canned creamed soup could be added to nearly any combination of meat, vegetable, and starch to create a meal presentable as original and fancy. Gelatin made salads. I grew up in a rockety time of change for food culture. In the 1970s, everything changed. Women stood in the stillpoint, as buyers, cooks, advice givers, and eaters.[1]

Iceberg lettuce gave way to romaine which gave place to arugula which ceded to kale: food writer David Kamp calls what happened since my childhood the "Arugula Revolution." The stirrings that transformed American food culture gathered from storms churning over far corners of the landscape. In the early 1970s, *Gourmet* magazine and food writers like James Beard and Craig Claiborne began schooling readers in fine dining. Julia Child had opened the educational front with French cooking, appearing in hardcover volumes and on public television. Child made preparation of fine cuisine accessible, posing whimsically as untutored home cook so we watchers could follow along and learn.[2]

The 1970s invented machines that would change kitchen habits. The Crock-Pot spent its first few decades undistinguished as a bean cooker until being rebranded in 1971. The microwave brought the jet age into the kitchen, looking fabulously futuristic before taking a ubiquitous blocky place on counters everywhere. The Crock-Pot and microwave addressed the same problem from opposite directions: how to have meals ready at dinnertime when cooks did not get home from work until just before, when cooks were working women who were no longer presupposed home all afternoon

---

1. Shapiro, *Perfection Salad*; Shapiro, *Something from the Oven*; Veit, *Modern Food, Moral Food*.
2. Kamp, *United States of Arugula*.

Good Things to Eat (Food)

because they were now at jobs that paid them. Another new tool, the food processor, cut in the opposite direction by putting elaborate projects into reach, making cooking a hobby.[3]

Food-interested folk who had nothing to do with each other in the 1970s came together by the 1980s. People who worried about the environment and how chemicals and fossil fuels harmed land were closely related to hippies whose food must be near nature. These could make common cause with those who did not want to hurt animals, while boycotters supported migrant farmworkers. From this crowd came health food and vegetarianism, an ethics and a politics too. My hometown abounded with people then called Granola Babes. In Ithaca in 1973 Mollie Katzen and her friends founded a shrine to meatlessness that yet endures, the Moosewood Restaurant, selling an exuberant crowd-pleasing vegetarianism with cheese on top of almost everything.[4]

The more purist strain of this to-the-earth movement came from California, marrying haute cuisine with peasanty aesthetics, gardener-chef types dressed in linen and holding a basket. Food tastes not only went deeper into the earth but circled all around it. American audiences schooled by Child in the rules of French cuisine got smitten by things Italian, and the Italianate cuisine birthed a generic Mediterranean diet mostly descriptive of California. Two mighty streams edged past haute cuisine in the 1980s: Italian and fusion. Fine diners were to seek not just Italian food but off-the-beaten-path dishes from a remote Tuscan village. Trendy Mediterranean food purported authenticity to up the ante. Status came with specificity. This new, regionally specific Italian food did to insecure eaters the deed that many other cuisines have done since. It took the diner gently by the shoulder, or not so gently, pulled the menu from his hands, told him that he was ignorant but could be taught to recognize what was true and right to eat, that he should not be satisfied by bastardized pandering versions and that his success and status as an eater depended on contemning Americanized foods and claiming only authentic cuisine. Ironically, this rightest-highest food often actually was *cucina povera*, the food of the poor, which the educated diner could esteem higher than the middling kind. Knowing your regional Italian (or later Indian or Spanish or Thai or Mexican) cuisines gave fine diners a perch to mock the red-sauce crowd from above and below. The

---

3. Kauffman and *Bon Appetit* staff, "How 1971 Changed."
4. Rothman, *Bun in the Oven*, 112–13, 123.

more lowly a sophisticated diner got, the more local in his cuisine preferences and ingredient origins, the higher would seem his tastes.

The second trend, fusion, domesticated exotic cuisines by glazing them first with a European or Californian gloss. Fusion reversed what happened to immigrants' cuisines the century before, the melting-pot dilution that produced canned spaghetti and chop suey, instead effecting a highly self-conscious mix of high cuisine. It was also opposite the *cucina povera* impulse, not stripping dishes back to their authentic forms but cross-pollinating to reimagine, which made them more American. Fusion prompted foodies to roam the globe for good things to eat. Now the Southern Hemisphere, now the subcontinent, now worries about cultural appropriation, now all in for Korean barbecue—the bar was always moving. The whole globe competed for the attention of our tongues. Americans wanted to eat the whole world, but only the best from it, trends trickling down because profits were to be had in selling fancy food not only to fancy people. Profits were to be had by letting everybody eat the best newest thing, and then when something became popular, letting high tastes move elsewhere. Starbucks started making everybody's coffee and then became insufficiently sophisticated for fine coffee drinkers.[5]

In ways zigzagging and contradictory, the transformation of American food nudged us to enjoy and justify, avoid and rationalize every bite in order to take only the best. Decades keep teasing out the contradictions in our efforts to eat what we want and feel good about it. Many imperatives crowd into every choice. We want food to make us healthy, which primarily means looking good and living long. We want what tastes good to be healthy but also be an indulgence, at the same time marking our conscientiousness. Historian Adrienne Rose Bitar argues that Americans use diets to recover a fictional purity or golden age. In practice, "good things to eat" and "good for you" more often than not are opposites. Worse, what is good for you in one decade might turn into something sinful by the next generation. Historians of American diets note pendulum swings from weight-loss regimens of grapefruit and cottage cheese, directed at particular problems like heart disease or diabetes, to wellness advice applied to everyone. Analyses of Americans' bad eating habits in this period fault factory farming and ultraprocessing, the food deserts and swamps that limit healthy choices for many and offer junk instead—burgers, fries, fingers, poppers, nuggets—whose impact is worse than going hungry. Malnourishment in

---

5. Finn, *Discriminating Taste*.

America now more often signals eating too much wrong food than not getting enough to eat.[6]

But what is "enough"? Nutritional advisors in the 1980s and 1990s tried to reframe the way we measure and count this with serving numbers and portion sizes. Counting is an obtuse way to approach food. William Atwater introduced the calorie to American nutrition in the nineteenth century, making food quantifiable in terms of energy output, as though that were all eaters expected food to provide. Vitamins boomed in the early twentieth century, science supposedly helping health by giving eaters something else to count. When one way of counting causes problems or proves imprecise, a new method is introduced. The urge to quantify surged with technologies that could be sold to count more things, disburdening dieters of keeping track by tracking everything. Forks that total up the calories in every bite have not swept away our conventional cutlery, but watches connected to smartphones keep tally of health data for many.[7]

Counting may be neutral as an activity by itself, but it reflects unfortunate habits and can make them worse. Counting suggests that our problem with eating is ignorance—we don't know what food contains or how much is needed—and that we would behave well if we just had accurate information. In 2006, journalist Michael Pollan looked America in the eye and said, the problem is that you do not know what to eat. Americans buffeted by one nutritional fad after another really did not know any more what was good to eat. That was the point of *The Omnivore's Dilemma*, and Pollan, an excellent diagnostician, also provided a solution, his seven-word mantra: "Eat food. Not too much. Mostly plants." Pollan was right about a lot.[8]

Suppose calorie charts or smart spoons could tell us what each bite of cereal, salad, or tempeh contained so that we would consume the amount sufficient to fuel the body and then stop. If the monitors told us we had eaten too little or too much, we would adjust accordingly. That correction would suppose that our problem with food were rational, that if we only knew the right information, we would have no dilemma. But lack of knowledge is not really our problem with food. The problem is wanting always to eat what we like and shun consequences, wanting the best bite and then justifying what we want, wanting to moralize our own diets by vilifying

---

6. Bitar, *Diet and the Disease of Civilization*; La Berge, "How the Ideology of Low Fat Conquered America."

7. Mudry, *Measured Meals*, 47–76.

8. Pollan, *Omnivore's Dilemma* and *Food Rules*.

somebody else's. Americans' eating problem is less a matter of ignorance than distorted self-awareness and too little wisdom.

EATING IN LIVED EXPERIENCE

In Junes my mother watched classified ads in the *Ithaca Journal* for announcements that U-pick strawberries were ready, under the column "Good Things to Eat." At the farm we walked all the way down rows to the back before squatting with trays in damp furrows between raised plants. The farm attendant told us smaller berries were sweeter. We picked the small ones but were not fooled. Of course it was better to get a big berry than a small one. Big ones are scarce. They weigh down the stems. They get their tips stuck in the dirt, making them more often the berries with the worm hole or rotten spot on the underside, fruit imitating life. The occasional whole, heavy, perfect berry, glinting metallic under the cross-hatch of seeds, shiny and smooth at the shoulders under the cap of leaves, that is a prize. Eaten warm right away, those berries are best, core pulled out of white hollow in center, a full-juiced mouthful. Second best are strawberries in strange shapes, fused ones or many-lobed. We ate and picked until baskets were full and we were itchy and sticky and sated.

To eat or not to eat, that is the question. When harvesting a row, one wonders whether it's better to wait and wash and slice and eat at home, whether it is theft to eat what has not been weighed and paid for. Eat, of course eat. My aunt, after she got born again, used to fault my mother for letting us steal when we picked berries. A fine casuist, my mother said the berry farm expected us to eat some. She offered to let the farmhand weigh us on the way in and out and promised to pay the difference. Eating your fill was half the point of going to pick.

In that dawn it was bliss to be alive, but to be young and eat was very heaven. Ithaca, New York, was a paradise of good eating, plentiful, ethnic, seasonal. In fall we visited cavernous apple barns, wooden crates piled full of Red and Golden Delicious, Macintosh, Macoun, Empire, Cortland, Jonathan, Mutsu, Jonagold, plus a barrel to tap for cider. On winter days my mother dropped us off at the golf course to sled or ice skate, packing hot milky cocoa in glass jars wrapped around with kitchen towels to hold in the heat. My siblings and I ate nearly everything that came our way. Sardines, sauerkraut, cabbage, caraway seeds, polska kielbasa, lima beans, but for me finding a raisin in something ruined it. Everything was about to change, did

Good Things to Eat (Food)

change, but I was just waking up to American food, and so could not tell what was new and what was normal, nor what belonged only to my little place and what the world just did.

I love to eat. I am good at it. But determination to enjoy it all became a problem. I wanted only good things to eat. My problem is our problem. What got me hospitalized later as sick for being stick-thin was not body dysmorphia or idolizing thinness, stereotyped teen-girl maladies, and it wasn't hating food. It was doing the same thing most Americans who can afford it are doing right now, striving to eat the best. Wanting to eat only the right things that taste best sometimes can lead to bad places. Sometimes it is better just to shut up and clean your plate, shut up your head and your tongue both.

Some gene for good taste could have come from my ancestors. Or it could just be that they were hungry all the time. Peasants turned family farmers prepared the ground. The best food was what came for peasant feasts, paska and nut horns and pirohi for occasions. Pirohi are the Slovak equivalent of better-known Polish pierogi dumplings, poor-people celebration food, starch wrapped inside of starch and fried in butter. The only properly Slovak food I learned from Baba was this feast-day food. What Slovaks ate day to day in the old country fell away. My grandmother thought I ate too much and occasionally worried to my mother that I had a tapeworm since I ate so much but was so skinny.

Since we usually visited Pittsburgh in summer, boxloads of produce came from farms in Ohio where her in-laws and cousins lived. Many times while she was peeling potatoes, Baba told how her father stored up potatoes in whiskey barrels so the family always had food to eat during the Depression. Potatoes loomed large in memory. She said often, we hardly knew it was the Depression, we always had food to eat and my daddy gave food to anyone who came to his door, tramps off the train who came begging, getting a roasted potato or hunk of bread. My mother also remembered her grandfather's potatoes. The October she was born, in the middle of the Depression, my grandmother gave birth to her a few hours after helping get that year's potato crop in. My great-grandfather had new Slovak arrivals often at his farm, helping them find work or settling disputes. He hosted people and fed many, throwing bushels of potatoes onto glowing coals and then, when they were blackened done, shaking the potatoes around in burlap bags to slough off the burned skin. My mother ate potatoes hot from the fire with farm butter melting over them and dripping down her arm.

Sometimes my great-grandfather also held over the flames a whole rack of bacon while the eaters were waiting for the potatoes.

One Pittsburgh summer we visited some Ohio relatives who may or may not have known that we were coming. That time it was close to lunch. I was crabby about the whole thing, riding in the hot backseat, mad to have to talk to people. I was cross about their featureless ranch house and the hours we were wasting. They led us right to the table. The hostess—a great aunt?—brought out a platter of corn that she had just fished from a boiling pot, butter-and-sugar, white-and-yellow corn. A plate of tomatoes already sat on the table. She put down salt and pepper. It may have been the best food I ever have eaten. Kernels full and crisp to the tooth, milky and juicy and sweet but not candied or starchy, glazed over with butter roughed up with table salt. Tomatoes were arranged in meaty slabs, incarnadine flesh with smallest scallops of seed-jelly around the edges. Tomatoes got salt too and needed cutting with knife and fork, and they left red putty on the plates. I understood a little why this Ohio would be hard to lose, why Baba mourned to leave.

If my mother timed the summer visit to Baba's right, we got to go to an amusement park in Pittsburgh once a year, Kennywood, on Slovak Day. Between roller coasters we did not eat corn dogs or sno-cones from park booths but stuffed cabbage in the Slovak Festival pavilion. The same things, roaster pans of kielbasa, of stuffed cabbage, of haluskis kapustu, showed up at weddings and birthdays and showers. When I visited Slovakia for the first time after I graduated from college, a cousin there made a treat to celebrate our arrival. He cleaned sticks and built a campfire, putting on the pointed end of each twig not a marshmallow but a lump of bacon fat.

Baba's food contrasted with what we might eat when we went to visit our favorite cousins and their kind parents. My aunt made casseroles and Hamburger Helper in a skillet, the thing that we called a frying pan, and she offered side dishes, cut corn or slivered beans, from serving bowls. Despite having fewer casseroles and serving bowls, my mother cooked as many mothers in those decades cooked. For thrift my mother cooked almost always, day after day and without fanfare. She set the table and the example, that the way to feed yourself well is to cook for yourself. We were very well fed every single day, almost everything from scratch, our hamburger unhelped. With few exceptions her food was always good. We ate a lot of soup. She knew what was good and told us to eat it. Most of the time she was right.

Good Things to Eat (Food)

My mother had few cookbooks. This by no means signals any lack in my childhood culinary education. She had a Betty Crocker cookbook and Peg Bracken's *I Hate to Cook Book*. I read the Betty Crocker cookbook often. I read it, I strolled through its cool, mannerly world of dining rooms and ironed napkins, observing its heroine, The Mother, in earrings and chignon with an apron tied around her swirling skirt, probably smelling like perfume. In Betty's world, women wrote shopping lists in looping cursive, they planned meals, they served soup as a *course*, they occasionally made Foods from Foreign Lands, and they sometimes prepared special dishes to tempt flagging appetites, a phenomenon I puzzled over. Who had to be tempted to eat? In Betty's world, women made cakes every day. I knew they did, because a whole section of a chapter demarcated "Everyday Cakes," confections that seemed no less elaborate and from-scratch than the special ones for holidays, since who, anyway, would rather eat a Yule Log or fruitcake than a Bundt with a tunnel of fudge?[9]

I also enjoyed reading the *I Hate to Cook Book*, which somebody must have given my mother as a gift because this was not her world either. The writer clearly was a very good cook and must have liked cooking enough to make fancier foods than what my mother's table featured, but mostly she narrated all the other things she'd rather be doing besides cooking and what a drag it was to have to pull out her casserole dish and sling hash. Mrs. Bracken's house was as strange to me and perfumed as Betty's, but different. Her gripe with cooking bore no resemblance whatsoever to the soup-pot counter-top sink-full that we helped my mother manage every day. While complaining over what she'd have to cook when her husband's boss came to dinner or flicking ashes off the end of her cigarette, Mrs. Bracken let me into a world of glamour, ennui, and silverware that I would later recognize as the problem that had no name. Why did Mrs. Bracken hate to cook? Maybe she was joking.[10]

The food movement and diet developments bloomed while I was a teenager learning how to eat only what I liked and stay skinny while doing it. That also seemed, still seems, what everybody else was trying to do too. I also had my very own revolution. In junior high I set three priorities for myself in summers: I wanted to be thin, tan, and smart. They were hard priorities to balance. Reading could distract from eating. Being hungry

---

9. The Betty Crocker cookbook has gone through many editions. I own one that looks as I remember it, *Betty Crocker's New Picture Cookbook* (1961).

10. Bracken, *I Hate to Cook Book*.

made concentration hard, a price sometimes I was willing to pay. I wish somebody had told me skinny was with me for the long haul, just kind of there, one of the attributes of the kind of body I got, like having wrinkly hands or prominent veins. That should not sound boastful. Other people have plenty of body characteristics I wish I had. Default thinness has made some things easier. I do not have to worry constantly about weight gain.

It would have been better not to worry about my weight at all. It would have been better to learn, too, that every bite doesn't have to count. I have taken a lot of delicious bites. But sometimes good taste has to be waived for politeness or haste or to avoid waste or for someone else's need. Every forkful does not have to be optimized. It would have helped if someone had told me, look, don't worry about being skinny. Some foods you just eat for nutrition or from hunger. You may gain a few pounds, it's fine. You don't need to do all that stupid stuff.

When I went for a physical after eighth grade, my weight had gone up since my last annual visit. One of the pediatricians in the office responded with this advice, "Don't eat any more French fries," and I didn't eat French fries for the next decade. What happened to me? No switch flipped in my head. No pound-goal dominated my weigh-ins since my family did not own a scale. No body goal ruled me either, although everybody else in my family was good at sports. I wanted to be thin because every American female wants to be thin. No originality there. I wanted to be thin *and* I wanted to eat the best food available. No originality there either. You can't stay thin if you eat everything, so you have to choose. I chose to eat only the things that I wanted and could budget for total intake. The food world of the US in the 1970s and 1980s was built for that kind of budgeting, recipes tagging calorie counts and women's magazines featuring a new diet in every issue.

Diets were exactly the opposite of what I was trying to do. The diets did exactly the wrong thing: script consumption. They required a lot of uninteresting food for the sake of health. Why would I want to eat dry toast and a boiled egg for breakfast, a skinless chicken breast and spinach for dinner, and ice milk for dessert? I wanted instead the donut, the ice cream cone, the square of lasagna, even if for the rest of the day and the next I had to starve to pay for it. I am describing what I thought, not what is right to think.

I was hospitalized for a little while for weighing too little. My mother had to take me to a therapist as a condition for staying out of the hospital, and the woman must have cost my mother a lot, an academic therapist who had done research on the history of anorexia. I didn't give the therapist much to work with. She smoked her way through our sessions in a small close room and when the fumes would make me tear up, she would decide that my crying signaled progress. The therapist theorized that perhaps eating was for me a way to control something, since adolescence and being fourth of five children in a divorced household gave me little else that I could control.

But I was not starving myself as a way to exert control. I was not starving myself as retaliation for family strife. I was not starving myself because I wanted to look like a model in a magazine or wanted to look good for boys. I was eating selectively because causal relationships exist between food consumption and body size, and I wanted to consume more than would be appropriate for my size, as nearly everyone does—the tapeworm apparently having deserted me by high school—and so I had to consume carefully to eat what I wanted.

Eating disorders can kill and maybe I had one. But I wasn't trying to do myself in. If no switch flipped to get me into this mess, none switched back off to get me out again either. Mostly what got me out of this phase of life was working in a candy kiosk in the mall and eating what the owners conceded was reasonable consumption of chocolate pieces and cashews for employees each shift. I regretted a little that I felt fatter from the candy kiosk but I ate a lot of chocolate. My normalized weight removed me from doctors' attention. I didn't get cured. I just ate more. Food is your friend, somebody told me, you don't have to be afraid of it. When my weight returned to statistical norms, thin but normal, the calorie counter still kept ticking in my head and for years I believed I could eat either lunch or dinner but not both until a friend told me that was stupid, so I started eating dinner even if I had already gone out to lunch with her. Then I ate breakfast, lunch, and dinner like a normal person, and nothing about my body changed very much. The calorie counter got shoved further back in the mental closet of obsolete appliances. I can still tell you calorie counts for most things if you want to know, but I would have to rummage around and blow cobwebs off that machine and I assume you don't really care about those numbers and I don't either.

Cooking also helped. I had been cooking for my family since about age ten, my turn in the chore rotation. Unlike thinking about eating, cooking requires obedience to the way things actually are, to matter and its properties, how things behave and not only how they appear in your head. The cook can participate in the glorious givenness of the world, that things come in seasons, that techniques yield different results. Treating things well in a certain way mixes your labor with creation and the result is good. Coming out of the thrall of counting and worrying about food, I quickened to creation, joined my craft to the raw materials of the created world. I made sourdough, coaxing yeast out of the air in a sludge of mashed grapes. I made puff pastry dough some nights in the years when I only had one baby. When the child was asleep in her crib I went downstairs and whacked butter with a rolling pin on the cold countertop, then folded floury paste around it over and over for a laminate dough, hundreds of layers. I whipped egg whites. I caramelized onions. I tossed sugar in a pan and caramelized that too. That was beautiful work, and a ticking calorie meter is not an appliance useful for constructing a laminate dough, or any of the other constructions.

WHAT'S STRANGE ABOUT EATING THIS WAY

American obsession with numbers and weight, fitness and thinness, presses against ever-raised interest in fun food, new food, the gourmet donut. In our lifetimes, not only profit-seekers trying to sell us low-fat high-sugar snacks have confused us. Our doctors, our experts, have done so too. Eaters were told by authorities that this thing was good and that thing was bad, only to hear five years later, no, that was bad and this was good, often without the authorities admitting the contradictions. I hate when people don't admit the contradictions.

My friends' mothers dieted with grapefruit halves and cottage cheese and burgers with no buns. But then somebody pointed out that the fat in the burger really was the problem, so back came the bun. But, someone else said, meat is what all our cavemen ancestors ate. But, someone worried, maybe all that meat fat is clogging our arteries. In the 1990s trans fats were revealed to be so dangerous that manufacturers were shamed into stripping them from formulas. Shortly after, wellness-minded people started cooking with coconut oil, the new blue-ribbon fat. At the dawn of the twenty-first century, health experts vilified carbs once again and gluten-free products bloomed briefly. High-protein paleo and keto diets lured people who could afford them, obscenely, while the foods keeping most of humanity alive for most of human history, bread, rice, pasta, beans, were cast as not only

Good Things to Eat (Food)

lowbrow but evil. Then, with even starker judgment, influencers and officials trying to make America healthy again declared war on seed oils and food dyes.

With food as with so much else, these decades delivered the sensation that right was wrong and wrong was right and nobody really could tell which. Americans absorbed wave after wave of changing dicta and reacted accordingly. After all that, Americans might choose, foodwise, to believe nothing. Or we might keep looking for someone to tell us what to eat—even if what we really want, deep down, is to trust someone to deceive us, to give over responsibility of choice to someone who declares, against the evidence of our own senses, that the indulgence really is the healthful thing. What we really want from diets is permission to eat what we like and act as though it has no consequences. Some diets do that even still. Food is often moralized. Eaters counter morality with morality. American grocery stores offer individuals lots of choice while profit-makers churn out chips and snacks designed for addiction.[11]

Food-movement gurus make a persuasive case that our food production methods are killing the planet and us, but for many of us it is hard to connect principle with behavior, especially when the same people who advise earth-friendly options first raised our tastes. The country and the globe hold a lot of people, and they need to be fed, and I am not sure all can eat the clean, gentle, local way. For millennia, rich people ate rich food and few people had the luxury of being overweight, while lowly foods and scarcity beset people who did not eat richly every day. In our transvaluation, poor-people food now is admired by rich people and poor people now eat richness previously reserved to the wealthy, but without the usual rule-setting by culture that built helpful limits into feasting, like St. Theresa of Avila saying we should fast when it's fast time and feast when it's feast time, and not confuse the two.[12]

Intentionally confusing fast and feast is Americans' self-inflicted wound, the 100-calorie pack of cookies promising dessert after every meal. That numerically rationed treat-everyday system is our problem. Most of us do not need counting to tell us how much to eat. Instead, we need to rebalance what we learn from manners, from appetite, from dimensions of teeth and mouth and hand, from the earth's limited resources and the obligation to share them. Novelty, selection, self-expression distinguish

---

11. Moss, *Hooked*.
12. Nestle, *Food Politics*; Silbergeld, *Chickenizing Farms and Food*.

the rich, who can display education through the health and aesthetics of choice. Even the best choosers have a hard time putting together parts of right eating: good taste and nourishment, ecology and convenience, what is fashionable and what is just. Some analysts exonerate the individual eater and blame systems, factory farming or advertising or capitalism, running a whole gigantic apparatus suckering the poor slob to upsize his fries. But people in other societies that are also subject to those systems escape the problems that strike American eaters.[13]

What's strange is that fancy food got normalized as spectator sport by the end of the twentieth century even while ordinary people stopped cooking. Home cooks purposed to make fancy food formerly found only in restaurants and special occasions. That project seemed dazzling at first but it burnt Mom out, who, anyway, was more often busy during her day earning a paycheck. What's strange is that cooking became hobby rather than daily drudgery for many adults, which left their kids ignorant of kitchen basics. Some stumbled upon kitchen arts later on their own through social media and acted like they discovered fire, which basically they had. What a surprise this all would have been to Mrs. Bracken, that cooking should be something to do for creativity and fun. What's strange is that conscientious twenty-first-century cooks discovered that the best food often was local and handmade from natural ingredients, a loop that connects high tastes and low ones but again shames the middle.

BETTER THINKING ABOUT EATING

The food environment my childhood met seemed to solve many problems people perennially confront. The future appeared to offer great abundance, nutritional knowledge, elevated skill in cooking, and delicious international plates rather than bland ones. Instead emphasis fell wrong in each category. Abundance got made by burdening land and creatures, maldistributing excess and manufacturing waste, feigning infinite resources available all the time. Americans came to expect the all-you-can-eat buffet. Bounty turned to harm when eaters took too much, gulled into treating glut as good portion or treat as staple, then erred in blaming the food itself or setting health

---

13. Writers like Michael Pollan and Marion Nestle locate responsibility in large-scale food systems, manufacturers and lobbyists and industrial feedlots. *New York Times* food writer Mark Bittman puts together systemic problems and personal agency in *Animal, Vegetable, Junk*.

Good Things to Eat (Food)

opposite to pleasure. Intemperance could be cloaked with a reduced-fat version. Nutrition advice may have gotten clearer but stayed misleading, easily manipulated and creatively misinterpreted. Delicacies from foreign lands got fused and remixed and plastic-wrapped. Cooks liberated themselves from kitchens to depend on prepared items, making farm-to-table an elite mystery. Leaning the other way would have kept the feast separate from the daily bread, could have honored better what land and hands made for the good of the body. It still can.

The Standard American Diet is sad, costly to produce and consume, but fun to eat. We abuse our bodies by eating what tastes good, even if what tastes good at the moment comes from a gas station. Loaded burgers and french fries taste good. We abuse the animals we shove down our gullets as fast as they can grow, demanding a chicken in every pot every day for everybody. We abuse the people who grow this food and slaughter it and pack it in plastic, the vulnerable workers paid next to nothing for brutal jobs, in order to keep drive-thru meals cheap. We want everything to be available all the time and in every place, strawberries year round and avocado on every toast, and then we throw loads into trash bins because we bit off more than we can chew or left those expensive greens rotting in the crisper.[14]

The reason some other places do better amidst their own variations of capitalism and global homogenization is that in some other places, cultural authorities remain intact. They keep hierarchies and rules, experts and ancestors blessing or banning, at least to a degree. A graduate-student couple from Bologna came to my mother's house for dinner once and brought their infant. To feed the child while my mother finished getting dinner ready, they stirred hot water into cereal flakes, as one does in America, and then the child's mother did what I guess she might do in Bologna, took a napkin-wrapped chunk of Parmigiano-Reggiano cheese out of her purse and asked to borrow a grater. She passed the cheese over the fine side of the grater and scraped the shavings into the child's dish, "so he gets the taste," she explained.

We need to get the taste, to learn to like what we are supposed to eat. We should eat certain things when they are in season and not at other times. We should learn how to admire what is in the market and what to do with it. We should cook some things exactly as our grandmothers did because grandmother may be still eating at the same table with the rest of

---

14. Child labor helps keep American food cheap. See Dreier, "Kids on the Night Shift."

the family. We should eat dinner sitting down at a table, about the same time our neighbors are also sitting at table. And if it is not a feast day, we should be thankful to be eating daily bread, not trying to get dessert out of a low-calorie package.

Allowing daily bread to be something other than daily feast would lighten pressure on the person who, in many homes, still assembles dinner: Mom. The others in a household perched on stools around the kitchen island, waiting for that meal to plop down in front of them, might protest that the job is no big deal. The market gave Mother electric appliances to help keep her at this post even after she got a day job, gave her packages from the deli aisle, Blue Apron, DoorDash. Health advocates are careful not to blame women's employment for ruining the American family dinner. True enough: Americans do not *have* to visit the drive-thru just because Mom and Dad both now come home from work about the same time each night. The fault is not Mom's but ours, sins of commission—our elevated tastes, always wanting new and best—and omission, the failure of somebody else in households to rise to this office, somebody besides the delivery guy.

For the dawn of the twentieth century, feminist writer Charlotte Perkins Gilman offered a biting critique of gender inequality and dinner. Gilman wanted women to have interesting jobs rather than seeing themselves as employed by their housework. In her book *Women and Economics*, Gilman cataloged the evils multiplied by mothers' cooking. Undereducated, most women could prepare food but not did not know how to choose what was nourishing. They fed their families on love, not science, so Junior grew dependent on Mama's biscuits, learning to equate love with the lumps of dough distinctive from his mother's hand. But biscuits made Junior a dull boy, constipated and stubbornly opposed to properly healthy foods. The solution to both problems—Americans' poor health and women's kitchen thralldom—was to sever the link between food and mother-love. Food should be prepared and eaten in institutional settings by scientifically trained experts who would deliver nutrition more reliably and also release women from the daily slog of chopping and cleaning up. Gilman wanted to give American women in cities modern apartment buildings with centralized dining and housekeeping. In her time, this meant something like a residential hotel. In our time, it means something like a college dorm. Large-scale institutional food delivery was the solution both to women's inequality and to ill-health by overweight. Contemporaries of Gilman's suggested other schemes, dining co-ops or trucks dropping off dinner or the hosting of big communal meals.[15]

Americans resisted, thinking throughout the twentieth century that this means of food provision was a bad idea. The nuclear-family dinner table was locus of love and togetherness, meat and three with a layer cake to finish. Postwar prosperity and mid-century gender roles doubled down on Mom's cooking. Betty Crocker showed Mom how to do it. To abandon Betty's world would be to deprive women of the opportunity to show love through deep knowledge of her beloveds' particular preferences and quirks.

I used to balk at Gilman's solution. I balk at scolds who say food should not be connected with love, that Moms should not comfort kids with cookies. Gilman and others doled out this advice before the phrase "comfort food" even was invented. I think Gilman is wrong about that. So much good is entailed in that handing over of a cookie, mother to child, here take this one, I made it just the way you like it, no raisins. But Gilman is right about so much. Our error is not in rejecting her prescription. We have accepted her solution with a vengeance. We have leaned hard in the direction of institutionally prepared food, something we pay to have show up at the front door. We have sprung Mom free from the stove but not from the duty of dinner.

My first child laughed with delight when she first tasted a slice of pear. It was about the most appropriate response to the universe that I ever saw. Food is for nourishment and enjoyment. Cooking and eating, we admire the astonishing match (mostly) between what nourishes the body and delights the senses, between labor and reward.

It is amazing, the match between the things that exist and our ability to taste them. Like a lot of other people, during the COVID-19 pandemic I lost my taste. At first I could taste and smell nothing, then I could taste mostly nothing except bad flavors. Peanut butter felt like wet cement and smelled of garbage. Scientists guessed the COVID brain was trying to rewire itself, making some mistakes along the way. It was a horrid but illuminating experience. I could not trust the evidence of my senses, say one thing was good to eat and another was bad, because I was not an accurate interpreter of sensory reality. I might think the thing tasted bad but someone else would be right.

The nuances of taste are much more complex than the counting of carbs, calories, pounds. The matter of what exists should amaze. Flour.

---

15. Gilman, *Women and Economics*; Hayden, *Grand Domestic Revolution*, 150–81.

Sugar. Egg. Suor Juana Ines de la Cruz, the Mexican nun-poet who argued for female education, teased her critics with "the secrets of nature that I have discovered while cooking," observing how eggs behave differently in oil and syrup, how sugar turns from solid to liquid in heat, noting that a person can philosophize while cooking dinner and, "As I often say when observing these little things, if Aristotle had cooked, he would have written much more."[16]

To worry first about how food will make us fat or sick, even to worry first about how to make it taste good, is to chew it up before looking at it, to suck food into the maw of our self-regard before appreciating its plain fact, to turn it into a tool before admiring the thing itself. Food is your friend. It doesn't have to be your best friend.

Michael Pollan boiled down a rule for eating to seven words. Inspired by his rule, I offer some rules even shorter. Six words: Behold, it is good. Enjoy enough. Or five words: Hands made this. Appreciate it. Or four words: Moderate serving, full pleasure. Or three words: Give thanks, eat. Or two words: Eat. Stop.

---

16. De la Cruz, *Selected Writings*, 43; Mazzoni, *Women in God's Kitchen*, 137.

Chapter 2

Continuing Education (School)

A CLASS CALLED "CREATIVITY" was mandatory in the middle school of our small-town New England school district in the early 2010s. This class was offered by the business department. In middle school the business department specialized in classes called "computing" but functionally equivalent to a 1980s course in typing. Business teachers spent much of their time showing kids where to put fingers on a QWERTY keyboard because homework increasingly was done online.

Creativity was billed as a different kind of class. Its contours were revealed during parent-information night. The teacher, qualified to teach typing, asked parents to stand on top of the chairs where their kids usually sat. While parents balanced awkwardly on the plastic chairs, the teacher commanded, "Look down!" and, crowing with enjoyment, told parents to stare hard at the carpet. "See how that changes your perspective!" The carpet, which had looked mottled beige, revealed a slight pattern when studied from higher elevation. If we were willing to take the next step, to get on our hands and knees to see the carpet at eye level—which, the teacher assured, students had done—we would see even more colors, flecks of reds and blues and brights spotted through the beige. "That's what we're trying to teach your kids in Creativity!" she concluded with a flourish. "Because the jobs of the future will be different kinds of jobs. Your kids are so far ahead already! We're training them for jobs that don't exist yet!"

A SHORT HISTORY OF AMERICAN LEARNING

No shortage of creative approaches has aimed at imparting knowledge to American kids. American children have learned in many environments, at parents' knees or at catechism, in the field or at a workbench. In the past, not all children had the luxury of schooling. Youth were needed instead as hands or feet for the labor of running a household economy. New England colonies established town schools in the seventeenth century in order to frustrate Satan, that old deluder, whose one chief project was to prevent God's people from reading Scripture. Literacy was necessity in early Massachusetts. In Virginia, Thomas Jefferson dreamed up a system of public schools in the eighteenth century. He wanted schools organized by county, the lower-level grades with broad enrollment to teach rudiments to the many, higher levels culling dullards year by year to yield smaller groups of better boys. In Jefferson's plan, after a few years at grammar school, each "best genius of the whole" would then continue education for six years, with "the residue dismissed." Minus the deadweight of that "residue," Jefferson would ensure that "twenty of the best geniuses will be raked from the rubbish annually" for study at public expense.[1]

Some colonies carried educational infrastructure into early US statehood, but the common-school movement revolutionized American education. Led by Massachusetts's Horace Mann in the 1830s, legislation required taxpayers to fund schools then required children to attend them. Advocates invested nearly messianic faith in the power of education. They designed common schools to foster democracy by bringing together rich and poor children, mixing backgrounds and social classes, though the vision was compromised from the start by racial exclusions. Some states not only failed to provide for Black children but banned their instruction. Common schools were to teach native-born children how to be good citizens and immigrants' kids how to be American. The nativism accompanying school-reform energies spurred some immigrants to build their own parallel system of schools, which Catholics did through the low-cost labor of priests and, especially, nuns.[2]

Common-school advocates saw education as indispensable for a self-governing people. After all, ordinary boys could grow up to be voters or even become president. Public schools aimed to inculcate a shared

---

1. Axtell, *School upon a Hill*; Jefferson, *Notes on the State of Virginia*, Query XIV.
2. Neem, *Democracy's Schools*, 1, 11–24, 150–72.

patriotism, habits, and hygiene in hopes that pupils would take those lessons on to home and family, to the public sphere and to the rest of life. American girls got instruction too in the nineteenth century, though not so directly for sake of citizenship. Alongside tax-funded schools, many private schools were founded, including female seminaries. School hands on the verities of a present culture to the next generation in hopes of shaping present and future. The common character of schools made them sites of bitter contention again and again, over religious instruction, over racial integration, over content of lessons in science and social studies and sex, because so much is at stake in how one generation shapes the next.[3]

In the nineteenth century, farm or family or military service might abruptly close a young person's school years. The reinvention of high school in the early twentieth century normalized secondary schooling not just for a few affluent young men or women. Indeed, more girls than boys were enrolled in high school in the mid-nineteenth century. In 1900 about a half-million teens attended high school, then two million by 1920 and over six million in 1940. The Depression reinforced the new trend since it made sense to keep young workers-to-be in school rather than releasing them into competition with adults for scarce jobs. Consequently, while fewer than 10 percent of adults were high school graduates at the century's start, nearly 50 percent were by mid-century and 90 percent of eligible students were enrolled. By century's end, the vast majority had completed high school, though with uneven rates across racial lines. Reformers debated making different curricula for students taking jobs right after graduation rather than heading to college. Vocational tracks got federal-level support in the 1917 Smith-Hughes Act, acknowledging that schools helped some students better by preparing for paths other than college.[4]

The expansion of high school highlights another rationale of American education. Citizenship was never the sole goal of common schooling. Its contribution to the American economy also has long justified public investment. In the early twentieth century, when fewer Americans would be employed in agriculture but more in trade and industry, mandatory schooling made economic sense. Future workers needed skills of literacy and calculation. America's factories and offices needed not only warm bodies, but

---

3. Turpin, *New Moral Vision*, 39–108.

4. Beston, "When High Schools Shaped America's Destiny"; Goldin, "How America Graduated."

men and women prepared with skills that made them able to fill those jobs, a public investment that paid off in economic growth.[5]

Expanded high school shifted the kind of education students would receive before and after it. Early twentieth-century psychologist G. Stanley Hall popularized adolescence as a developmental phase needing particular encouragement. To prepare rising students for the challenges of grades 9–12, the first junior high schools opened in 1909, Ohio leading the way. Later, educators created that strange beast, the middle school. Conviction that tweens need more support, plus local exigencies of racial desegregation, turned junior highs into middle schools.[6]

Middle school tries to dignify the indignities of the most awkward years, incubating inanities among hormonally volatile bodies striving for recognition. The unique selves in middle school usually turn out to prefer the same few name-branded clothes. The kids who seamlessly adopt the uniform and its behavioral attributes, who play a sport or two and perform passingly well in class, are the kids who write the rules. In the early twenty-first century, middle-school curricula prioritized anti-bullying while constructing ideal breeding grounds for bullies, fencing in a crowd of phone-toting children who formed an unmediated market for people to sell them the stuff, paid for by their parents, by which to build a unique self.

By the middle of the twentieth century, high school completed education for most Americans. In its second half, a high-school diploma became the ticket to yet further schooling, as college became a popular stop on the route to adulthood. In contrast, a tiny percentage of elites attended colleges in America's earlier centuries. Most colleges were founded to educate the colonies' ministers and officers and to cultivate the sons of the prosperous. Harvard started in 1636, the College of William & Mary in 1693, and most of the colleges that would form the Ivy League were established in the eighteenth century. America's residential colleges created a distinctive norm, built to form character as well as impart knowledge, with religious and reform priorities giving them shape. Courses in natural theology and moral hygiene presupposed that reason could know things about the world and God, and that those spheres of knowledge connected.[7]

---

5. Labaree, *Making of an American High School*, 1; Goldin, "How America Graduated," 2.

6. George, "Early Success."

7. Delbanco, *College*, 1, 55; Mintz, *Prime of Life*, 17–66.

Continuing Education (School)

In the middle of the nineteenth century, revivalism and entrepreneurship multiplied the sprouting up of small colleges, first in the east, then west with the plough. Like common schools, colleges were imagined as vehicles of social improvement. Ohio once again distinguished itself. Oberlin was founded in Ohio in 1833 by inspired Presbyterians, a college integrated by sex from its beginnings and two years later by race, a rare combination on the globe then. In 1862, during the Civil War, the Republican-led Congress invented land-grant universities in each (Union) state to teach especially useful subjects, agriculture and engineering, funded by the citizens of that state. Decades later, American institutions got remade in the image of new universities in Germany. New universities were structured for research, for pushing forward the boundaries of knowledge rather than handing on old wisdom, in newly founded institutions like Johns Hopkins (1876) and the University of Chicago (1890). Even hoary old colleges refashioned themselves. Harvard's president, Charles W. Eliot, dismissed traditional curricula and advanced a system allowing students to select their own elective courses.[8]

Research in universities could yield benefit to both society and economy. War made that point especially clear. By depleting student bodies of young men, the world wars also opened more space for nontraditional attendees, including women. Military application of research, especially in science and engineering, pulled government dollars into public and private institutions. If wars temporarily reduced the number of young men filling seats in university classrooms, mid-century peacetime restored those numbers many times over. The aftermath of World War II invited in many Americans who previously might not have planned on college, mostly young white men. The 1944 Servicemen's Readjustment Act, nicknamed the GI Bill, sought to reward and train soldiers returning from war rather than putting men back into job markets. New cash and students grew American universities in scope and footprint. The flood of students and government money warranted reshaping. In the 1960s, Clark Kerr made influential reorganization of California's state system. He constructed a three-tiered system of public institutions offering different educational levels and prestige and proposed the "multiversity" to extend the function of higher education into American society. Desirable jobs began to presuppose a college degree, a fact carrying social implications as well as economic ones.[9]

---

8. Delbanco, *College*, 82–85.
9. Thelin, *Going to College*, 116–19; Eisenmann, *Higher Education for Women*; Thelin,

If in earlier periods college was, to Andrew Delbanco's description, a "quasi-penal" environment where parents sent their boys, campuses in the 1960s became arenas to test out new freedoms. In the 1960s colleges stopped acting in *loco parentis*, dropping curfews and housemothers. Though later decades imposed their own rules governing sex and speech, college still invites young people to imagine it as an arena of liberation. That, as much as its instructions or credentialing, has made it seem an indispensable feature of developing adulthood.[10]

Because a college degree appeared for a while to be the pass to comfortable middle-class adulthood, justice required broad extension of that access. As with common schooling, American principles might even demand that college doors be open to everyone. Aid to racial minorities in the 1960s was reframed as promoting diversity after the US Supreme Court, in the 1978 *Bakke* decision, disapproved affirmative action. Though the court forbade race-conscious admissions outright in 2023, consensus advocated opening higher-education access to diverse students.[11]

Efforts to expand access to college came from other directions too. Standardized tests were first promoted as instruments of broadened opportunity. In 1926 a version of the SAT was piloted at Harvard, and mid-century the Educational Testing Service incentivized admissions departments to require applicants to submit test scores. Lyndon Johnson's 1965 Higher Education Act expanded federal financial aid. The Pell Grant program in the 1970s gave grants to lower-income students. In 1975, some institutions agreed to use the same procedure for admission, forerunner to the Common App. In 1992, FAFSA became standard for students seeking financial aid. President Bill Clinton proposed turning college into a universal part of American young adulthood. Though funding was comparatively modest, the social assumptions behind his 1996 plan were ambitious, Clinton commending that, "our goal must be nothing less than to make the 13th and 14th years of education as universal to all Americans as the first 12 are today."[12]

History of American Higher Education, 138–41, 277–80.

10. Delbanco, *College*, 18–19.

11. Delbanco, *College*, 35; See *Regents of the University of California v. Bakke* (1978); *Students for Fair Admissions, Inc. v. President and Fellows of Harvard College* (2023); Thelin, *History of American Higher Education*, 347–50.

12. Lemann, *Big Test*; White House–National Economic Council, "Raising Student Achievement."

Continuing Education (School)

College has not become universal. But many more Americans have wanted to go to college than could afford it easily. Presuming that college is what people do to become middle-class adults, more American students apply. Of the many students who apply, many bid for few spaces in a few high-status places. Meanwhile, smaller colleges with lots of space available struggle to survive, dreading the demographic cliff of white high-school applicants. Universities that carry more prestige are swamped, welcoming more applicants so that they can exercise the privilege of turning most of them down. At these selective schools, applicants have a vanishingly small chance of admission at a school of their dreams.

But *maybe* they might get in, hopeful high schoolers think. The hope of long-shot applicants that perhaps they might be the ones to slip into their reach school fuels frenzy, especially by students who have resources to play admissions games. By the hard logic of meritocracy, applicants already privileged can pad their leads, hiring tutors and finding activities to list on college forms. As this century opened, high schoolers had gotten busier, joining teams and clubs, inventing leadership posts, starting companies, achieving world peace in order to make themselves the kind of persons that elite admissions committees want. Political philosopher Matt Feeney raises due concern that highly selective colleges should not so dictate standards for American childrearing, squeezing kids to generate appealingly unique selves to wedge into the few negotiable slots at prestige colleges. Many are called but few are chosen. We may not all get into Harvard but Harvard wants us all to want to.[13]

LEARNING IN LIVED EXPERIENCE

My grandparents did not graduate from high school. My mother's dad, the eldest son in his family, left school to help sell farm produce and later took a class to learn welding. My grandmother returned to Ohio from Slovakia when she was a teen and knew almost no English. She was placed in a classroom with young children. She stopped going to school as soon as she could. She knew how to do all the work of a household. Mass was in Latin and Slovak, and she knew what the words were supposed to mean.

My mother's happy memories of school mostly come from their neighborhood near Pittsburgh, when wartime work brought the family back to Pennsylvania for good. They lived in a two-bedroom apartment

---

13. Feeney, *Little Platoons*, 213–50.

with five kids in McKees Rocks. In the evenings, by her report, women sat on their stoops and talked while children played marbles and hopscotch. A rabbi and his family lived next door. Four saloons stayed open on their block. Their apartment building sat near St. Mark's Roman Catholic Church, containing a world in a city block, with a rectory, elementary school, and a convent for the sisters who staffed the school. Miraculous, woman-powered engines of Americanization and progress and uplift, nun-run Catholic schools in American cities provided for the education of many like my mother. Church collections funded the schools and parents in the parish sent children there. My mother learned the usual things in school: math, geography, spelling, grammar, science. For high school, she caught a bus and streetcar across town to Mount Assisi Academy, run by the same Franciscan sisters from Slovakia. Their girls' basketball team played half-court. The most distinguished high school girls got crowned May Queen to honor the Blessed Virgin Mary.

Her parents sent her older brother to college in nearby Latrobe, Pennsylvania. When my mother decided to go to college too, she had to pay for it herself. Work was to enable school and not the other way around. Her bachelor's degree qualified her to be a school teacher, but whatever the diploma signified for her, she was not done with education.

In contrast my father reaped the benefits of several land-grant universities. When he got out of the army he taught chemistry in high school. Cold War energies funded science education, lest the Russians outmatch us, and shoveled federal cash to those seeking advanced degrees through the 1958 National Defense Education Act. My father used this kind of money to get a master's degree at Wayne State in Michigan and then a doctorate at Cornell in Ithaca, New York. He studied goat lactation and did radiation experiments. His research profoundly affected the course of our family life, whatever it did to expand the range of human knowledge.

We came to Ithaca on his account not hers, but there were few seasons during her part-time university job when my mother was not also taking Cornell classes. More of those were Russian classes than anything else, language and literature, Pushkin and Gogol. For years our car was a rolling language lab, narrated by the cassette-tape dialogues of Sasha and Masha, a fact mortifying to me when my friends rode with us. My mother took other classes too: constitutional law, German, Italian, art history, psychology, pomology, vegetable crops.

Continuing Education (School)

My mother taught me how to read. In a green spiral notebook she wrote columns swapping out letters, C-A-T cat, B-A-T bat, P-A-T pat. I sat next to her at the kitchen table and moved my finger across the letters. When I went to kindergarten at Northeast Elementary, across the street from the apartment building where we lived, our first day featured a worksheet with the letter A, capital and lower case. That surprised me because I already knew A. I read my first book myself when I walked home from kindergarten one day and the doors were locked, my mother not home yet, so I sat on the building steps and turned the pages until the end.

My first grades blur together, spelling tests, multiplication tables, the sheer worksheetyness of the days. Our family's unspoken understanding was that good grades were expected but not special or important. I did, and as far as I could tell my classmates also did, what was in front of us not from a sense that we were optimizing our intelligence or advancing toward a career but putting effort in a project like doing a puzzle, being handed piece by piece a frame showing how the world is put together. Twice a year a siren prompted our classes to crouch under desks or hunker down in hallways for nuclear bomb drills. The day was broken by lunch and recess. Recess, what hell in a half hour, a period always winter and never Christmas. To be fair, winter recess was much better than green-grass recess, because things could be built out of snow, and one could join the squads of kids who were building forts or snowmen. In green-grass season I spent recess mostly wandering around trying not to look alone. Sometimes I could join a knot of girls picking flowers from weeds at the wood on the edge of the playground that we were told belonged to the Iroquois. We feared that it would be granted back to them, which would be just though inconvenient.

In classroom afternoons it was the custom for teachers to read aloud while waiting for the clock to run out on the day. In fourth grade my teacher read aloud from *Bridge to Terabithia*. Several chapters before the end, our teacher started to cry, sniffs here and there and then thick-choked swallows. She was reading a sad part. We listened, quiet enough, until our teacher slapped the book down on the desk and shouted, "Don't you people understand what's going on here?" She saw our quietness as incomprehension. She proceeded to summarize the plot. Some kids snickered. What my teacher said is what teachers often want to say to students: do you get the point? If you got the point you'd be reacting differently. Do you even deserve this treasure that I am trying to give you? Don't you people understand?

Disoriented

The upper-grade classrooms in Northeast School opened on to the library, which meant that the school library was always available, which meant the whole world was available. My life has been this way ever since in principle if not physical space, lived walking through the library, books before and around any space marked by formal instruction, books to provoke, console, stretch. I read *Peanuts* comics, *Narnia* books, *Little House* books, *All of a Kind Family* books, *Anne of Green Gables* books, Nancy Drews, Bobbsey Twins, *Johnny Tremaine, Mrs. Basil E. Frankweiler, The Phantom Tollbooth, The Witch of Blackbird Pond.* I read all of the *Biography of Young Americans* books on the shelf about girlhoods of famous American women, who were not that many and frequently were girls who grew up to be wives of famous men. I walked home from school with a book open in front of me most days. I did look up to cross the street, usually.

The sound most memorable from Northeast School, besides loudspeaker warnings against snowball fights, was Harry Chapin's song "Flowers Are Red." Ithaca schoolchildren could sing that song by heart whenever it rang out, at lunchtime assembly or at the downtown festival, that ballad about a creative child whose brilliance is quashed by a teacher who wants him to color inside the lines. Ithaca schoolchildren knew the refrain well enough to belt out, no! Ithaca schoolchildren were supposed to reject conventional forms, to trample received wisdom, not conform to some rule. I was willing to not conform, though my personality pulled the other way. As an Ithaca child, the command to trample received wisdom was itself such received wisdom as I had.

Grades six through nine I spent at junior high. Junior high sorted kids who were stronger at math from the English-and-history kids, where I numbered myself. I disappointed the high expectations of the algebra teacher, who judged me against the precedent of my older, smarter siblings. This teacher took a sabbatical to Japan and came back with the idea that pupils in her class should bow when she entered and should start and end our class period cleaning the classroom, wiping desks and emptying the trash. I was not great at algebra. I competed in spelling bees and won a thesaurus from a local bookstore with my name engraved in the front. My mother bought me a book called *Spelling Your Way to Success*, a title implying those words fit together. My classmates said I was most likely to grow up to be an English teacher, but that was compliment rather than prediction. We did not have any notion in junior high what result would come from continuing to like to read or spell.

Continuing Education (School)

It never occurred to me that being good at English and not so good at math meant something about my future, that is, my future employment. Privilege delayed comprehension but my obtuseness did too. I heard people tell kids that while they were in school, school was their "job." Maybe blissful ignorance was a perk of being a good student in a time and place when nerdy girls were not regularly assigned ambition, ignorance that permitted never calculating what learning might yield in terms of future salary. In high school I once went with other smart girls to a local college for a recruitment day about math and science, informing us that girls weren't excluded from those fields anymore. Careers awaited female chemistry majors and engineers! That day-long invitation to connect a field of study with work came and went because I was not good at those particular subjects.

It is possible that some of my classmates had ideas of the causal connection between biology class and what they hoped to get paid to do as grown-ups, but I did not. Being a good student meant learning things so you would know enough to keep learning the things you were supposed to know as a grown person. Schooling gave goggles for clearer vision, cabinets to place the strange objects that would materialize in life, decoder keys for new languages. Teachers let us in on how the world works, catching us up to what happened before we woke up, telling us the inside jokes. My older siblings told me Western Civ was boring but I liked it, doorstop textbook with yellowed pages of tiny print and the occasional black-and-white photo, Plato to NATO when that still felt like the end of the story.

Passing between classes on the windowed ramps, I felt a lag and a longing, wondering how to fill the long minutes of being alive. Thinking seemed a plausible way, that and reading. Lunch periods I often spent in the library. I discovered the Sunday *New York Times*, which I worked my way through by sections during the week. The newspaper administered the sting of having entered a conversation late. The point of going to school seemed to be to make oneself qualified to read the newspaper as an adult, to learn now in order to know what was what when required to know. I stumbled onto book reviews, the lazy person's way to learn a lot fast. I read the travel section and found places I wanted to go, mostly Italian hill towns.

Enough people in my university-town high school planned to go to college that I assumed that was what a person did. I thought about college irrationally, as most high schoolers do. I started as a Hotel Administration major. I had to take a class that trained us in making spreadsheets. Mostly unable to get the columns to line up properly, I assumed Excel was something nobody would ever need to know. That first semester, the only class I had outside of hotel school was Western Civ. That history course led me out of hotel school into the College of Arts and Sciences, which felt like I had snuck into something grand. One day in late September I sat under a blazing maple tree and read my assigned pages from the *Confessions* of St. Augustine and reached the part where the saint steals pears. Behold, I thought, I am in college. The reading felt to me what college is supposed to be, the sky clear blue and the sun filtering through the leaves, and Augustine right about the way humans are, woe is us and thanks be to God.

Midway through the first semester I was told to choose classes for the second. That atlas of dreams, that annual buffet the course catalog, was a book I loved, the thick, paper-profligate catalogs colleges used to publish before these went online. In print the catalog offered something awesome, page after page of classes students could take, cryptic notations distinguishing ones offered in fall or spring or in alternate years or with prerequisites or cross-listings in other departments. But how to choose? Midway through that first semester, I had this revelation: I will never learn Urdu. The catalog brought this revelation, our liberal arts institution where any person could pursue any study. How exhilarating. (My university's pretense that I could pursue "any study" was not strictly true. At this university, the academic discipline in which any person could find no study was religion, thanks to the vision of founder Andrew Dickson White.)

Clarity was provided by a rush of competing desires and priorities. Confronting my limits as a learner—sleep, shyness, spreadsheets—thrust reality back. Some things must be chosen and some left aside. Some omissions would become regrets, some omissions would be leavened with relief that other people did the thing that I left undone.

I loved being an undergraduate. I went to classes and did homework. I loved getting to know people through shared ideas, the way people introduced themselves wordlessly by the books on their apartment shelves. Most of the time, learning made me feel like I knew less rather than more for having learned it. In college my head got used to two new feelings. The nicer was the exertion of trying to understand, that pleasant strain near the top of the skull stretching to hold something worthwhile. The other feeling came often and still comes: the feeling that I had actually been wrong the whole time about something I thought I understood. Ohio turned out to be one of these things. To get through a class or an exam, to make an argument about anything for which one has usable coordinates, this set of readings,

Continuing Education (School)

that set of dates, one had to assume as true what never really should be assumed. Literally every sentence in each lecture could be its own lecture. Participating in class discussion means sauntering forth in ignorance and letting yourself be contested.

I decided to study history. History concerns both the big and the little, the grittiest granular and the widest arc. Historians need the particular—the exact word in the document, the stained shirt, the post-beam, this treaty, that vote count, this street address, that potsherd—to make an argument about something as a whole. Learning to think historically felt like a magician's trick or a scientist's. History lifts the curtain to let show a little corner, to show how things got to be the way they are, how things could have gone another way. Most of the time I felt like I barely understood anything, though in graduate school I took to walking around naming things in historical context the way a botanist identifies plants. History was a way to know, not the only way but a serviceable one.

I did not learn either Excel or Urdu. This a partial list of what I learned in college: that the two-party system was the bedrock of American political stability as long as it lasted; that the cathedral was a metaphor for premodern Europe, that giant open space with a whole people acting as one body, and the Enlightenment made us individuals, your own butt in its own chair and your soul stuck with itself; that Henry Adams knelt before the dynamo but would have worshipped the virgin if he could have. I notice literature is missing from the list. Science and math also are mostly missing. My professors were great lecturers, makers of sophisticated arguments clothed in illustrative anecdotes and primary sources Like other people, I forgot some of what I learned in college. Much got built into the framework of everything else I learned thereafter. College gave me more than I knew to ask for. What a glory to entrust to a young person, that her chief responsibility for a period is to learn things that excellent people had shaped their lives around knowing and bade me to share. I hereby apologize to my college professors, as I apologized to my junior-high algebra teacher, that I did not take their instruction as far as I could have, that I don't have laurel wreaths to lay on their tombs in tribute of how much I love what they taught me.

I graduated from college with a head full of things that made me wonder what else I was misunderstanding. I also wondered what I was supposed to do with all the stuff in my head because if I died it would all vanish into dust. Where would it even go, what I knew about Martin Van Buren and Mannerist painting? The two ways of getting it out seemed to be either writing it or telling someone. In 1990, for the first time ever, I was done with school. What summer job I had turned into a normal job because I was still at it in the fall. Before I graduated, a favorite professor had told me that I should only go to grad school if I were sure, since graduate school was not sitting around and eating bonbons.

I started a PhD program later because I thought the point of it would be for learning more things, maybe reading more from the most prime of the primary sources or old texts in the original languages. I alone am to blame for the mistake. My graduate study in history was a pre-professional credentialing program, as much directed to future employment as law school or medical school, maybe more so since in those fields there actually are jobs into which credentialed graduates could be slotted. In the first week our US history graduate class was told that two-thirds of us would be dropped after the master's degree. My advisor was working on a book arguing that New England Puritans held in productive tension their interiority and active striving, the individual conscience and common weal. I was persuaded. Still, graduate school was a grim slog of feeling inadequate, no bonbons at all. When I told my advisor late that first winter that I thought about dropping out, he told me I would feel better as the weather improved, which was a funny thing for one fan of Puritans to say to another. He was right that Virginia spring is beautiful. Like a stowaway on a ship boarded because I thought it was headed someplace else, I figured I had to obey its manners until I got to port.

WHAT'S STRANGE ABOUT LEARNING THIS WAY

In principle, American schooling should be so good. Public officials dedicate funds to learning, even averring that no child be left behind, a wild pledge given how recently school segregation was law in some states. Teachers bend over backwards to engage children, fill gaps in safety nets physical and emotional for the kids who show up in their classes. Kids have schedules cleared for schooling, no factory shifts competing for their time when their job is school. The internet promised to put more information into the hands of babes than was to be found in the most stuffed of university libraries, all the information in the world accessible to everyone. The prosperity, security, diversity of the United States in the years conveying me from start to finish in school offered all these goods and we might have seen their yield.

Continuing Education (School)

Less yield comes than might. Between my schooling and my kids' school years, some things changed. My kids started school in a small-town system in Massachusetts serving mostly college-bound families. The younger ones finished in a big midwestern high school. Their classes taught what state standards dictated. In the range of American public schools, my kids' schools were decent. Decent, in that lots of students performed at grade level, with low likelihood of gun violence, with no rotting trash. Some days were fine. They had to write a few papers, take some spelling tests, figure equations. They tried musical instruments. Still, it was mostly a drag, seven-ish hours a day to learn not very much. The most noticeable feature of my kids' schooling was the colossal waste of time. When my first child started first grade already knowing the tasks set as the year's goal, learning to read and write, the teacher rebuffed requests for extra activities. Kids basically all catch up to the same level by third grade, she told me. She asked whether I wanted the child to be smart or happy, as though she or I could choose one.

Curricula ever boasted the new and relevant but usually seemed no more effective, or less, than the tiny-print textbooks I used years before. For a few decades literacy instruction turned away from phonics and favored "whole language" or "sight reading" methods, no more C-A-T cat practice. My kids got lists of words to memorize, a literacy method that always erred by withholding the key of knowledge. My children had US history practically every other year, a never-ending loop making the same old stops, Jamestown and Plymouth, Salem witchcraft, the Stamp Act, the Revolution, the Civil War, and then on to somewhere in the twentieth century, World War II, sometimes the civil rights movement. They learned less about the rest of the world than they should have. In teaching US history, I found high school graduates still didn't know what the Stamp Act was.

What is strange is that adults invest so much into something young people often seem not quite to want, something whose value adults further diminish when they clumsily justify it for future wage-earning. My kids were told constantly that they could grow up to be anything they wanted because that mindset boosted girls while muting gendered scripts. When asked what he wanted to be, my young son said he wanted to be a robot. He may have misunderstood the question. Or he may have been prescient. Besides telling parents they were training our children for jobs that didn't exist yet, teachers' single most oft-made claim was that they made learning fun. Elementary-school teachers seemed obligated to stud every academic exercise with fun, daily doses of rewards and treats for very modest accomplishments.

Safe and fun: the moral range of public school is narrow, vigilant on a few points, tyrannically tolerant on the rest. Through the twenty-first century's first decade the highest goal was safety, daily reinforcement of rules for bike helmets and seatbelts and peanut-free lunches, and no firearms in the house. My kids learned that nobody has the right to impose morality on anyone else but also that smoking cigarettes was about the worst thing a person could do. And no bullying! Early twenty-first-century schools tried to reduce the harm students inflict on each other, forbidding certain insults and safeguarding sexualities. But there are many reasons a student might feel miserable in her own skin that are unrelated to sexual identity, and many idioms of insult violating no speech code but salting wounds, and many ways to enforce hierarchies and favoritism even in earnestly egalitarian schoolrooms.

Between my kids' schooling and my own, testing and technology touched everything. Proponents of testing and technology proclaimed both would benefit especially kids who tended to be left behind. National initiatives, like the No Child Left Behind Act (2002) and the broadly enacted Common Core standards (2010), alongside states' individual programs, multiplied the days of standardized testing in public schools. Teaching to the test is gripe and reality for teachers and kids. But damage done to learning by technology is far more dramatic, especially from technology that came billed as progress. Promised as a portal into the cosmos, dazzling equalizer offering riches of knowledge to children in slums as to princes, computer technology was supposed to improve everything about school.

Computers changed nearly everything. Much did not improve. Learning management systems replaced occasional report cards with daily updates. One-to-one initiatives pushed instruction onto screens, technology officers beaming as they thrust tablets into the hands of every child as though no one ever dreamed kids would use screens for things other than learning. When cell phones found a place in children's pockets, schools sometimes made rules that phones could not leave lockers during school hours. Many schools quickly abandoned those uphill battles. Often enough, teachers welcomed phones as substitutes for clunky calculators or computers. Like other cultural arbiters, schools are culpable for embracing cell phones when their dangers were obvious. A reckoning with schools' culpability should come alongside the new restrictions students have to obey. But

Continuing Education (School)

visionaries of another sort now want more such tools and not fewer robot teachers and AI solutions yet to come. Parents and school boards might be warned by precedent. Technology shredded students' attention spans. The jobs for which technology was touted as dazzling means and ends did not materialize quite as expected. Jobs of that kind might be taken by robots soon anyway.

The costs of strange things in K-12 education come bundled with the democratic goals and social attributes of it. But the costs of what is strange about college come itemized and accrue interest. Prescribing college for everybody stained college with the same flaw that turns kids off to mandatory K-12 schooling, but worse. College is not within grasp or desire of everyone. But an American economy shaped by the college-for-all ideal makes college seem prerequisite to a nice life. Kids whose parents have nice jobs and nice lives usually don't wish to give those things up. College-for-all skews socially viable options, contemning vocational training. The college application process is a burlesque of mismatched expectations, incommensurate desires, self-inflicted anxiety, bait-and-switches, delusions of grandeur. Through their applications, students yearn to be prized for their own unique selves while admissions departments see them as pieces to compose an incoming class with the group profile admissions officers choose.

This mismatch is what's strange about the way Americans approach higher education. Mismatch jars the process at nearly every stage, between what kids are primed to want and what parents want to pay for, between what colleges offer and what students hope to get from them. Some young people consider choosing a college approximately the way they might choose a Halloween costume or vacation destination or spirit animal. Hopeful high schoolers are not primarily to blame for the way these choices are imagined. Probably many colleges could be a good fit for any particular kid. Some choices are hardly choices, a few dominant brand-name institutions pulling applications like flies to light because their prestige is its own reward.

Americans may affiliate themselves with higher education for reasons unrelated to academics. Sports are the tail wagging the dog at some large universities. Introduced in the nineteenth century, college sports imitated the physical pursuits typical of Oxford and Cambridge, rowing and running, to fill out a muscular ideal of the college man. In 1972 Title IX of the Education Amendments barred sex discrimination and advanced women's equality in college sports. Television made college football and basketball a flood of revenue in college budgets and experience. Those and other activities do not always put students on their best behavior. Observers of American higher education sometimes quip that students who went to college in early America behaved as badly as students do now, maybe even worse, eighteenth-century boys rioting or dueling. Maybe students have always been unruly, but students have not always been so large a demographic, nor college the default activity for this period of life.[14]

Students may want a good college experience without really knowing what that should be. Parents want their children to be safe and have fun and graduate with a degree that repays the investment. Colleges offering rich material, especially in the humanities, get downsized because students may not perceive their appeal, colleges sometimes failing to describe what they do well, like a badly translated restaurant menu. Faculty want students to want what they offer not least because their lives are permanent exhibits to the significance of those things. Some college-shopping parents sniff at classes taught by adjuncts. Disapprove they should, not because their children are being shortchanged by adjuncts' instruction but because universities are as guilty of labor exploitation as fast-fashion stores are. What is strange is how much more extracurriculars matter to customers than do curricula. What is strange is that students go into debt for a degree aimed at a job and salary, though college should do much more for them than that.

BETTER THINKING ABOUT LEARNING

The education my childhood met seemed to solve problems that people perennially confront. Americans were given enormous opportunities to learn, so much made available in principle to so many, study made fun, unbounded knowledge to be pursued as far as wished for its own benefit and the good of the world. Instead emphasis fell wrong in each category. Opportunity became unattractive because mandatory, appearing to favor equality but in practice evading it. New technologies might have opened the world to more learners, delighting discovery and advancing common good by shared knowledge. When school was a thing to be assumed and dreaded, it had to be made fun, disappointing expectations since school ultimately had to serve future work. College can be enjoyed in many ways

---

14. Delbanco, *College*, 17–19, 70; Thelin, *History of American Higher Education*, 21–23, 177–82, 208–11.

but can also distort work and learning, can cost a lot and not only by financial measures.

College can be great, but I have to acknowledge that the best schooling in my kids' lives came in preschool. In preschool, life and learning were inextricable and interdependent, as were discovery and delight. What they learned was satisfying immediately and enabled what they would learn ever after. They were taught that the world deserved their attention. Teachers presumed kids did not know much yet and kids basically agreed. Some kids learned faster and others slower, manual and intellectual achievements valued together, the scissors grip and the alphabet. Teachers assumed parents wanted to share appreciation of what kids learned. After preschool, most teachers did not seem much enthused about my kids' learning. That my kid, or all the kids, should be dazzled by stars and sea or enchanted by a person in a book did not much appear to be part of the school day.

What lies on the other side of a thought experiment where children would get what they sometimes say they want? What if they did not have to go to school, could not go even if they really wanted to? In 2020, COVID played out that experiment. Remote learning revealed how small a proportion of the school day actually is filled by instruction. General disgust with remote learning reduced confidence in screens' effectiveness and stretched the gap dividing richer from poorer students Fights over schools' masking and distancing mandates exploded into other nastier controversies and animosities. COVID made visible the insupportable, contradictory priorities Americans pile on their schools.

Homeschooling went mainstream in the pandemic since everybody basically had to do it. Shutdowns made parents whose kids went back to school newly aware of what their kids were learning and newly thankful that somebody else was taking care of it. Long shutdowns in some districts made parents avid to get kids back into those buildings. Even kids themselves begged to go back to school, to see their friends or to get out of the house. COVID demonstrated that what Americans mostly seek from school is something economic, work related. It is a place to keep kids safe when parents are at their jobs and a place kids get qualified for the jobs they will hold in the future.

But the point of school is not primarily to equip a young person to earn a wage. Lots of other justifications for learning are better than that one: developing the self, shaping character, loving truth, loving one's neighbor. Even when rationales must be earth-bound citizenship is a better one than a kid's future contribution to the GDP. American schools, warts and all, can teach kids something about their time and place and how it got to be, reach for a common good and habituate them to look for it.

Readers may imagine various obstacles to achieving ideals of learning. Some children can take advantage of what education offers, some can but won't, some lack opportunity, and some only come for the extracurriculars. Learners might be reminded what school is for and what costs—individually and socially—are imposed on all of us when those goods are rejected. Remembering that in some parts of the world public schooling is not universal and girls are kept out of it might help remind readers why education should be thrilling. We don't celebrate schoolchildren on the other side of the world primarily for the sake of the jobs they will have someday. School is simultaneously downpayment for a better life in the future and evidence of an actually better one right now. What a high accomplishment it is for a civilization to mark off a season of life where growth of the mind takes precedence over labors extracted from the body.

Every generation judges American schools wanting, though with new species of failure. Some complaints about American schooling spring from conflicts between different goods, between play and performance, between equality and competition. Schooling can feel zero-sum even when one seeks the common good. Resistance can be petty, polite, or ugly. Sometimes, the way things work out, one kid can't get a seat in the best teacher's class because the neighbor's kid did; one kid's misbehavior means someone else's kid can't concentrate, and all that before college admissions when rejection letters name the problem out loud, that there is no space for one mother's child because a huge pool of others competes for the same seat. Parents who arrive early, who save the front row at spelling bee and school play and graduation, find ways to turn egalitarian policies to their own kids' benefit. In a way they are doing the right thing, though it is not always clear whether justice demands that they not do these things or that everyone should be doing them.

Public schools are a civilizational achievement. All should have opportunity. Schools are supposed to boost democracy by giving opportunity to each plus a sense of shared good to all. In practice, poor and rich kids get sorted, Black and brown and white kids get sorted, into separate neighborhoods and separate schools. Common schools cannot overcome the unruly opposing energies kids bring in, the awkwardness of growing bodies and the crooked timber of humanity that turns some kids popular and others marginal, some voted homecoming queen and others taking hits in the bathroom between classes.

Kids may resent school because they imagine it as pulling them away from what they otherwise rather would be doing, the fun they otherwise could be having. When American public schooling came to be, what many kids otherwise would have been doing was going to factory or farm work. A child who resents schoolwork because he imagines the alternative as snacks and video games would understand the options better on public schooling's original terms. If sitting still at desks writing sums or sentences seems unattractive to children, they might take tips from my junior-high algebra teacher and start classes instead with cooperative labor.

Higher education is a high civilizational achievement too. Not all young people should feel pressured to go to college in order to secure good jobs and lives. College defrauds when its goods are figured mostly in terms of entertainment or credentialing. It's a ridiculously expensive party, if that is a person's reason for going. For those who choose to go to college, fewer should beg dazzle-brand universities for seats at their little tables. For those who want what they do well, smaller colleges and universities provide a lot of learning. Many things can be learned on one's own. But to read books in community, to have one's mind changed, and to love others around ideas are gifts that American residential colleges give generously. And still, so much worth learning will go unlearned, even by most disciplined learners, a fact that merits some weeping and gnashing of teeth, on behalf of Urdu if not Excel.

Chapter 3

Seeking Fortune (Work)

IN JUNIOR HIGH I had a friend who lived in a big house on a wooded lot with a two-car garage. In spite of her noisy dog and three younger brothers, her house was always clean. Passing through the doors was entry to another world with stylish furniture and a faint whiff of her mother's perfume pervading all. Her mother registered to me not much differently from other friends' mothers except for a distinctive piece of crockery she kept on her stovetop. She had a spoon rest that said, "For This I Went to College." The closing punctuation might have been a question mark or exclamation point. I should remember, since I puzzled long over that artifact and what its slogan could mean.

If you understand the slogan right away, you occupy a different social place than I did. My family did not own a spoon rest. A spoon rest, what is that? I thought maybe the decorative spoon rest was its own answer to the question posed on it: I went to college for this, to marry someone wealthy enough to set me up comfortably in home and kitchen so I could have a decorative thing on which to place my wooden spoon. Or, I thought, it was possible that the spoon rest was intended as literal in a different way, perhaps if the owner had majored in food science or hotel administration, so spoon rest was a kind of continuing-education item. Or perhaps the spoon rest was ironic, suggesting that a woman who went to college expected to be employed in much more glamorous and high-paying work outside the home, and thus it was with wry surprise that she found herself in the kitchen stirring a pot—for *this* I went to college?!

By now I know how the spoon rest was supposed to be interpreted. But the ideal connections between college and "this," or between time and money, family and paycheck, have never been clear. They have not been clear to lots of Americans either, or clear in prescriptive literature about what was briefly called work-life balance before the implications of that phrase got embarrassing.

Picture books for children sometimes present a phenomenon called seeking your fortune. Stories imply that when the time comes, this is something people to do to grow up, a mandatory opportunity. Though the activity itself is a little obscure, from pictorial representation I learned that seeking your fortune entailed tying your belongings into a cloth and knotting this bundle at the end of a stick that you held over your shoulder, and then going out. Pigs are not the only characters in children's literature to do this thing but they display the paradigms well. Take the famous three. They all apparently found "a fortune," symbolized in building materials for their first homes, which present another aspect of grown-up independence: one can choose whether to make an easy or labor-intensive way for oneself. The pigs reveal more about the new lifestyles they bought than about their actual jobs. Where did they get those sticks or bricks? Finding one's fortune appeared to mean leaving home and having an obligation to build one's own dwelling. Beyond that, the responsibilities were unclear. Also, the gender of the three pigs is indeterminate. Marriage seems not to be equated with their adulthood launching, so I assumed they were male.

The three pigs' adventures are not mostly intended as a primer for adult vocations. But twenty-first-century children have many, many prompts to careerism raining all over their young years. My children were asked repeatedly what they wanted to be when they grew up. Describing what they wanted to be meant imagining an ideal future self in terms of a job title. In the United States, the linkage is tight between identity and work, though I grew up in a time when teachers in social studies classes had to explain that in the past, persons named "Smith" used to forge iron, a fact my schoolmates and I found silly. My kids were taught that children, like the pigs, were supposed to grow up to be what worker they wanted to become.

Women my age, Gen X women, supposedly grew up knowing that the world was wide open, that one could write one's own ticket, that women could be pilots and doctors and CEOs and so should prepare accordingly. I did not prepare accordingly because women's work did not look like that to me. At my college graduation, the commencement speaker told graduates to find something they loved to do and get somebody to pay them for it. The idea was strange then. It has not altogether passed the test of time.

A SHORT HISTORY OF AMERICAN WORK, ESPECIALLY FOR WOMEN

The prehistory of work can start in the garden. In the beginning the first man and woman were assigned care for each other and land and creatures. After they ate forbidden fruit they were not supposed to eat, toil became hard and subject to futility. Women's work had special connection to children and pain associated with them (Gen 1–3). Work could have spiritual benefit, as some in Christian traditions have pointed out. St. Benedict (480–547) blessed both work and prayer in monasteries. Medieval social divisions subordinated those who work to those who pray or fight, but Protestants from the sixteenth century on elevated work as expression of love for God and neighbors.

These ideas of work need noting because the Europeans who settled America brought them along. In Anglo-America, in principle, in the beginning, everyone worked. Two builders of early settlements let themselves be observed working the land, Virginia's John Smith (1580–1631) and Massachusetts's John Winthrop (1588–1649), setting good examples by their work in the fields. Agriculture as work defined European settlers in contrast to Indigenous peoples, whose habits of hunting and cultivation settlers disapproved. New England colonies embraced famously disciplined ideals of labor unto God, the Puritan work ethic taking shape in institutions, laws, and manners. In eighteenth-century Virginia, Thomas Jefferson (1743–1826) figured that the people laboring the land were "the chosen people of God, if ever he had a chosen people." Ideals about labor were undermined by the unfree labor Americans cultivated alongside their ambitions to self-sufficiency and private property. Slavery fueled the economy of the new United States even as it betrayed commitments to liberty. When states in the north and west abandoned slavery as the nineteenth century advanced, free labor defined political positions and regional identities in New England and the Midwest. Free labor produced that busy hum of activity that Tocqueville admired on the Ohio side of the river, the fertile land producing more because it was better tended by people theorizing that

Seeking Fortune (Work)

work was better than idleness and then putting on display the fruit of their exertions.[1]

Industrialization expanded other kinds of labor in the United States. When machines displaced craft production, workers in factories struggled to organize to seek better wages, hours, and working conditions. Though ethnic and racial rivalries and state resistance impeded them, unions developed. In the post-Civil War period came the National Labor Union and Knights of Labor, then greater success in the 1880s by the American Federation of Labor. Corporate violence and strikes early the next century, plus Depression-era radicalism and economic hardship, strengthened unions. The Congress of Industrial Organizations got founded in 1935. The federal government was intermittently supportive of collective bargaining in the postwar period.[2]

Factory jobs with union-negotiated wages made middle-class lives for many Americans mid-century. The decline of industry in the late twentieth century rescinded those opportunities, manufacturers taking plants overseas and jobs offshore, automation replacing tasks formerly performed by humans. The hollowing out of industrial America looked like creative destruction in parts of the economy, new businesses sprouting tech and biotech jobs sometimes from the very ashes of old industrial sites, in sleek lofts located in old brick textile mills. Some new jobs seemed lucky, tech work that broke conventional office rules and rhythms. Companies signaled transformation by banishing suits and ties and offering amenities like fancy free meals and table tennis lounges, perks for clever people in exchange for extended workdays. As the twenty-first century opened, the new tech jobs long prophesied were being invented, jobs where smart people made crazy money creating apps or putting commerce online. Some workers turned 24/7 availability and skill sets into bigger jobs funding well-styled lives. For others, disintegration of old office rhythms made work insecure, more flexible but tough to turn into a living. After the 2008 recession, college graduates had a harder time cashing in on the deal that somebody should pay them to do something they loved doing anyway. The gig economy was praised for entrepreneurship and creativity, but gigs can eat a lot of hours before they yield a living wage. We may mock the old world where Millers made flour and Bakers made bread. In our world too,

---

1. Innes, *Creating the Commonwealth*, 64–106; Jefferson, *Notes on the State of Virginia*, Query XIX.
2. Dubofsky and McCartin, *Labor in America*, 163–81, 245–70.

careers pin one's personality to paid tasks, identities cemented and polished by self-branding.³

Women work. Women always have worked. Historians tracing the progress of women's work in the United States emphasize this fact, in part to establish, contra 1950s television shows, that work is the norm rather than the novelty for women. While many women in the past did work hard for pay, or did work hard without pay because of enslavement, many American women have always done substantive unpaid work in their own homes too, except women excused by class. Housework done without electricity was strenuous, requiring more than one set of hands and strong arms to accomplish, therefore employing those model working women, domestic servants.⁴

Women always have worked. In farming families from early American settlement, women labored around garden and hearth, often collaborating with men's labor. Early industrialization at first recruited female participation, bringing the work to women in piecework systems, sending out shoes or garments to assemble for pay at home. Then industrial experiments in New England brought women into the workplace. Textile mills employed girls and young women, surplus labor from farm families whose households began purchasing rather than producing domestic items. Industry opened many more jobs to women later that century, garment businesses and glove-makers and canneries employing females, often at lower pay. A few nineteenth-century women also won fame as teachers and writers, artists and reformers. Other women defined their status by *not* working. For middle-class families where men went out for salaries in office or commerce, the home became configured as a sanctuary away from market exchange, one source of the mythology that American women historically have not dirtied hands with labor. Nineteenth-century separate spheres for men and women made more freshly obvious an old split between the sexes, that women would be launched into adulthood by getting married not getting a job, that seeking one's fortune meant seeking a husband.⁵

By the early twentieth century, cities offered new spots for women's employment, handling sales in department stores and clerical tasks in offices. When World War II drew men to battlefields, Rosie the Riveter types

---

3. Juravich, *At the Altar of the Bottom Line*; Gershon, "I'm Not a Businessman."

4. Kessler-Harris, *Women Have Always Worked*; Kessler-Harris, *Out to Work*; Strasser, *Never Done*.

5. Hayden, *Grand Domestic Revolution*; Rowbotham, *Dreamers of New Day*.

did their part by taking posts in factories. They did their part again after the war by leaving jobs to make room for returned servicemen. The postwar period energized later myths of the stay-at-home, non-working mother. College-educated women languished with nothing more challenging than carpools and bake sales and shiny kitchen floors, Betty Friedan reported. Friedan's *The Feminine Mystique* in 1963 diagnosed a nameless problem, the emptiness felt by housewives who were supposed to be satisfied by the leisure postwar affluence had given them but would have been better off with a job.[6]

Even amidst this season of stay-at-home moms, the US labor market had begun an evolution leading to revolution, economist Claudia Goldin argues. Goldin surveys the transformation of American women's work from nineteenth-century educated women who had to choose either career or family, to phases of twentieth-century evolution where women would put these together. First came women likelier to work when single ("job then family"), then a transitional group who might work later and in higher numbers without career plans ("family then job"). Women in that age cohort did not expect to spend whole adult lifetimes working. For such women, having a job became normal because it was necessary. The watershed came in the 1970s. Goldin marks that decade as revolutionary in how the economy would employ women and how women would shape their adult lives as earners. College-educated women might prioritize employment first and then decide whether to have children ("career then family"). Law helped, the fruit of Johnson-era civil rights legislation and executive orders forbidding sex discrimination in the workplace and establishing fairness with the Equal Employment Opportunity Commission. Science helped, contraception separating sex from childbearing so that phases of life could be sequenced.[7]

Women from the 1980s on planned for work differently and imagined its role in their lives differently, and formed adult identities through their work. These women did not have to choose work or family but could do one then the other. In the 1980s, the adulthood ideal did not even require sequencing seasons of life. Career and family could occur simultaneously. This was startling news. It had to be announced to people. I learned these glad tidings in childhood on TV in a commercial that aired during my grandmother's soap operas. This advertisement used a character to sell

---

6. Friedan, *Feminine Mystique*.
7. Goldin, *Career and Family*, 21–33.

the Enjoli fragrance, the shimmery blonde female who could bring home bacon *and* fry it in her pan. The woman in the commercial could be breadwinner *and* housekeeper. She was a mom too. And sexy! The ad jingle reassured viewers that this woman never let her off-stage husband forget he was a man, either, and she still smelled good after she put the kids to bed and went to slip into something more comfortable for the next shift of her twenty-four hours on duty.[8]

Women's rights movements could have taken many different turns in the United States. The way choices played out for work was neither necessary nor inevitable. The historic women's rights 1848 meeting in Seneca Falls, New York did not predetermine that equality in the twentieth century would be proven in the sphere of career. The revolution at full crest in the 1990s offered a promise called "having it all," which meant that social approval endorsed women's desires for work and for family, both things together. "Mommy Wars" became bitter battlefields of the revolution in the 1990s, when motherhood and full-time careers turned out to be less easily paired than some had hoped. Prioritizing just one of those seemed to obligate denigrating women who had made opposite choices. Sometimes motherhood appeared to be at odds with work—one's children getting in the way of work, or desirable work regrettably keeping one away from one's children—but work itself became nonnegotiable. With other milestones of adulthood unclear, being finished with school and having a job turned into a key marker of American adulthood for women as for men.[9]

The fork in the road on the way to seeking one's fortune, deciding whether to be a mom or something else, did not have to run paid employment on a road that led in different direction from the way to family life. Historically, the fork in the road does not present itself that way to men. Jobs give access to real power to do worthwhile things, to win respect, to earn for agency and independence. If the goal were mostly money, other measures could have gotten money into women's hands, mothers' pensions or guaranteed incomes or some other redistribution. Historical experience explains why work and family got set in opposition for women this way, but the two goods are not in principle opposites. Many other goods of adult female life could have been in placed in competition with motherhood: eternal youth, love affairs, the life of study, consecrated celibacy. In

---

8. Goldin, *Career and Family*, 30–3; See one version of the Enjoli commercial on YouTube at https://www.youtube.com/watch?v=N_kzJ-f5C9U.

9. Hays, *Cultural Contradictions of Motherhood*; Crittenden, *Price of Motherhood*; Slaughter, "Why Women Still Can't Have It All."

recent decades, childlessness became a socially legitimate decision made on grounds of personality or habits even before climate worries made childlessness seem conscientious. That choice is rarely counterpoised to work, because everybody works.[10]

It seemed good that women could have choices not previously available. If women wanted to have children, they could do that. If they wanted to work, they could do that. Choice evaporated from mainstream cultural scripts for work for women by the end of the twentieth century. By the end of the twentieth century, middle-class American women tried to "have" it all, work and family together, education and self-understanding driving them to the former while the latter was nice if you could swing it. Not that women sashayed smoothly into boardrooms. They had to contend with sexism and discrimination, working nine to five, a trajectory that was supposed to feel liberating. Belatedly, individuals and society at large had to rethink how women's new career choices affected everything else, like dinner. Despite a brief rash of conspicuous opting out by some college-educated women, the turn of the new century pressed women to lean in, as Sheryl Sandberg insisted, to a life defined by work.[11]

Leaning in was the charge for men and women, since the twentieth-century revolution in work came not just in one realm but in two, women's roles and the position of work in a post-industrial, globalized, neoliberal United States economy. Work got bigger, swelling to absorb one's whole life if in some seemingly contradictory ways. In some sectors work became "greedy," Goldin explains, when more high-status jobs demanded more of the employees who did them, more in-office time, near-total time on call. Men and women can choose more or less demanding jobs, but the demanding ones tend to be the higher paying ones. The demanding ones need more hours, social commitment, and availability, and they tend to reward men, single or married, and women without children. Totalizing work generates wealth unequally and inspires burnout, even among some doing very well in that world. Some college graduates with Gen Z sensibilities began to turn their backs on this package.[12]

Then the world changed again. COVID disrupted America's work habits and exposed features we had come to take for granted. The pandemic demonstrated how deeply women have been integrated into the nation's economy. COVID advanced remote and hybrid jobs and temporarily

10. Skocpol, *Protecting Soldiers and Mothers*, 424–524; Boushey, *Finding Time*.
11. Sandberg, *Lean In*.
12. Goldin, *Career and Family*, 9–13.

honored low-status essential workers. Post-COVID, evidence of Americans' dissatisfaction with work routines abounds, from the Great Resignation where many left jobs, to quiet quitting, where workers kept them but did less, to emptying out of office spaces and regional residential patterns shifting in response to digital nomads. Post-COVID, pressures come to return work routines to pre-pandemic shape, but AI glimmering on the horizon portends the end of many jobs.[13]

Women always have worked. But should everyone always work? Should women now work because they want to or because they have to? What else might women want instead? How should work undervalued by the market get rewarded? Is everything work: exercise, keeping friends, marriage, parenting, Christmas?

WORK IN LIVED EXPERIENCE

What counted as work for men and women used to be different. What counted as labor for my grandparents was harder than what the postindustrial economy would pay their grandchildren to do. In his off hours, as leisure, my great-grandfather ran the large farm my mother remembers. My great-grandfather and my grandfather worked in factories and belonged to unions. Unions not only made a good living possible for them but advanced their belonging in American political communities. My grandparents came to live in McKees Rocks, the site of a successful strike in the pressed-steel railroad-car industry in 1909. Before dawn each morning when my grandfather went to work in the factory, my grandmother packed his black aluminum lunchbox.[14]

My grandmother liked the kind of farm work she did with her father when she was young. She broke her back falling off of a wagon while taking in the hay, a story she liked to tell when her grandchildren tried frailty as an excuse to escape work. In her late nineties, when she could not move much farther than to her chair, my aunt gave her yarn and the crochet hook and she made dishcloths. When her eyesight failed, she kept crocheting, long chains that my aunt unraveled at night, winding the yarn back into a skein to be redone the next day. My grandmother said hard work was her secret for long life.

---

13. Alon et al., "Impact of Covid-19."
14. Lichtenstein, *State of the Union*, 82–83.

My mother's first job after high school was in a lumber company office, where she put her shorthand to good use. That, plus money she saved from playing the accordion at beer gardens on Saturday nights, allowed her to send herself to college. After she graduated and got married, she took a job teaching school until shortly before the birth of her first child, grounds for resignation. The kids in my mother's classroom cried when she left them.

The job she had most of her life, working as secretary at the office responsible for a university's student-discipline policies, was means to an end. Left alone in the town where my father's study brought us, with unreliable child support and five mouths to feed, she took a part-time job for a meager hourly wage. In hindsight my family praises this as her far-sighted plan to secure tuition remission for kids she could not otherwise send to college. It was that. It was also more immediately what paid for the roof above our heads and the groceries on our table. My mother typed, transcribed hearings, met with students. She provided magnificent if momentary service in the lives of some of these students, who had to look my mother in the eye to report what stupid thing they did while drunk. In the summers my mother got food stamps because we all were underfoot and she didn't go into the office.

My grandmother's work fit well with expectations for women in her era, and my mother's jobs made sense in terms of her cohort, as Goldin identifies it, women who ended up working a lot due to exigencies. My experience is less representative of my demographic cohort, non-exemplary in word and deed, though it may count for something as providing an angle for dissent from American work culture.

My first job in high school was at a candy kiosk in the mall. One summer I worked in an office, filing and typing. During college I worked at the dining hall and catering. A few summers I interned, that is, worked for no pay, at a political campaign and an office in Washington, DC. My first real job was in one of those Washington offices. I lived with an aunt and uncle because the salary was too small to cover rent. The boss of the office where I worked put in very long hours and had a very young child whose daycare routines my officemates and I overheard when she talked on the phone about them. Women at the daycare taught her son how to brush his teeth and how to use the potty. I wondered what relationship one would have with one's child if someone else taught him how to brush his teeth. The office was a fraught place whose prestige did not compensate for the tedium and stresses typical of office jobs. People seemed frustrated, which puzzled me because the television workplace comedy had not yet made this fact universally legible. I was advised that sticking out a job like this would provide an upward step on a ladder of advancement, but neither the goal nor the ladder seemed attractive after a while.

Quitting my first real job felt dramatic. I went to work for even lower pay at a policy journal. It was a lovely job. The job was to read manuscripts, enter edits, and typeset the articles. I learned a lot about how hard it was to make government policies achieve their desired effects by reading articles illustrating inefficacy. It was the first job I had where status rested on the untabulated work that one did in one's off hours. Persuaded though I was that many government policies fail to achieve their desired effects, I didn't have in mind any particular policies that I wanted to damn. I was in no hurry to leave the journal but failure to produce an article of my own shortened my tenure. I decided to go to graduate school in history. Neither of my Washington post-college jobs paid much. Both were places where it mattered to have ideas. Both jobs more or less confirmed a hunch I would never shake, that the kind of work I liked doth not a career trajectory make. That did not make it not worth doing.

I didn't know to look for a trajectory. Growing up to be a female physicist or lawyer never looked much more plausible to plan for than growing up to be movie star or tennis pro. All these could be possible for people with unusual talents and lucky breaks but they were not what most girls should anticipate. I did have living testimony of women working—to wit, my mother—but her job was a negative side-effect of divorce. It was clear that had she a choice, this job would not be it. The women I knew who had families with luxurious homes mostly did not have jobs, for *this* they went to college. These exemplars included many of my friends' parents, my mother's church circle, especially those whom my mother called "faculty wives," whose husbands were what she called "rich professors," a figure of speech I have never heard again. Since I later followed a career trail in a field where most find a wasteland awaiting at trail's end, the professors' wives familiar from childhood did not seem to have the worse arrangement.

Betty Friedan's problem was never native to me, since my mother had a job but also had plenty beyond housework to fill out her capacities. Other moms I knew did lots of things unpaid, in church, or helping refugee families, or taking care of grandparents, or managing gardens and solar-energy projects. A 1970s girl might wish that more options were open to women should she ever have to work, interesting jobs that paid well, but probably not wish for work itself. Having a career seemed to me a little like landing on a game show. You might win. Most people didn't. I grew up thinking that success as an adult female more likely meant *not* having a job rather than having one, not because I was lazy but because few jobs seemed actually available and those were not desirable except for their paychecks.

In the 1980s and 1990s while I was not paying attention, my nose in a book and my seasons measured in semesters, getting a job switched from option to entitlement to obligation for women. Long schooling is more than sufficient excuse for why I did not understand this in time. What I studied in grad school, New England Puritans, compounded the confusion. Puritans are great on justifications for meaningful work. They held in tension a bunch of principles that seemingly cancel each other out but nevertheless all must be upheld at the same time, puzzles often casually referred to as a "typical Puritan double bind." Puritans had typical double binds about almost everything: work, sex, monarchy, money, education, farming. Studying Puritans presented me with a double bind of my own. I arrived at grad school to continue my love of learning but discovered that its one chief purpose was to credential me for a job. Getting the credential required fitting oneself with an extremely specific kind of knowledge and binding one's sense of self to that very specific thing, so, for example, I am the person who knows Puritan catechisms. In pursuit of a credential, a graduate student is what she publishes about what she thinks. Getting a teaching job with this credential requires willingness to teach subjects related only tangentially if at all to the very specific knowledge that is one's personal claim to the credential. My years of study yielded a credential to get a job but there were very few jobs. This situation was bad in the 1990s and became bleaker with passing decades. What I learned to do well at graduate school is not of much market value. I discovered soon after that other people thought my education only was justified if I "used my degree." I used my degree when my first baby was about a year old because we had to make house payments.

The culture of work I entered when I finally left school and acquired small children looked like this: all adults were supposed to aspire to interesting jobs. Men were trained for interesting jobs that would earn money for things they wanted to buy and for the benefit of their dependents. Women, meanwhile, also were trained for interesting jobs that would earn money for the things they wanted to buy, but in order to get to their jobs women had to pay somebody else to take their children. Children, meanwhile, were supposed to play. Part of child's play could be playacting future jobs or doing activities in service of college applications serving future jobs, but children were by definition not responsible for any useful work in the present, since their job was school and school was supposed to be fun.

The culture of work when I entered it looked like an upward curve of progress. Fewer people had to do back-breaking, breath-stealing work because machines could take that beating instead. Education promised cleaner, nicer jobs, socially useful in their output and better paid than the old work. The country seemed to promise more jobs like these because the United States was moving from an industrial economy to a service economy to an information economy, people making money by doing things for each other and being smart. For the first time ever, women also could do these interesting jobs if they wanted.

WHAT'S STRANGE ABOUT WORKING THIS WAY, ESPECIALLY FOR WOMEN

Jobs offer the chance to decide what to be by deciding what to do and what thereafter to buy. American women still don't work exactly the way men do. Women's earnings in the 2020s don't match men's dollars, glass ceilings impede promotion, and motherhood penalties stunt finances long-term. But the scope of the change in women's work is far more startling than its breaches. Whereas some men were hostile to female employment in the past, either because of competition or implied critique of their inability to support a family on one wage, twenty-first-century men may take for granted that a wife works because otherwise, as a young man said to me, she would be freeloading, and what would she do with her time?

Men and women both now bind tight the relationship between sense of self and economic worth, the equation of who one is and what one does. Women might even be more motivated to defend that equation because they were so long shut out of good jobs. Arguments about women and work often run in the same worn grooves, the binary of motherhood and careers, pay equity and childcare, as though those were the only pertinent questions. Advocacy for women's work makes distinct promises whether emphasizing social or individual imperatives. When social reasons are prioritized mothers are told, the economy needs you so get your children out of the way in order to get to work. When individual reasons are prioritized mothers are told, get somebody else to watch your children so you can do your thing. The combination of these imperatives sounds worse than each alone: get your kids out of the way so you can serve the economy, which is where you will find fulfillment.

Seeking Fortune (Work)

Another sorry consequence of pressing identity into work and sending all work to the market is to strip value from work done without pay, much of which has been historically women's work. In the wake of 1970s social changes, some women were inspired to reframe the value of their work by calculating according to market rates all those never-done services moms managed. Wages-for-housework campaigns tried to itemize what it would cost to pay someone else for all the underwear folded and shirts taken to cleaners. Some women dislodged from their labors by divorce or budgets turned into characters called displaced homemakers. They did not get fired but had the value drop out of what they were doing. Clubs sprang up offering new skills or resume-writing classes to help displaced homemakers enter the job market. Studying this shift, sociologist Susan Thistle reports an illustrative quip of one bachelor, that he didn't need a wife because he could always just buy a larger supply of clean shirts and underwear.[15]

In the late twentieth century, other people less resourceful or harder to please than this bachelor discovered that when women left home to go to jobs, there was no one standing by at the ready to staff the parts of life that women had managed before. Even after they took jobs with hours and responsibilities like men's, women still ended up with much of a household's shopping, cooking, cleaning, budgeting, and scheduling. It took decades of living with this reality to name it the second shift and to redistribute it, his and hers. Failure to plan for this situation was a stupendous if unsurprising failure. Or, it could be argued, as Heather Boushey does, that employers intentionally built an economy around the housewife as uncompensated "silent partner," a support staffer whose activity is prerequisite to big employers' human resource management.[16]

What is strange about American work is how much we let it shape identity. What's strange is the priority we give to productivity, the tendency of higher earners to work more rather than less. What's strange is that women have been grafted onto this package deal just when its merits were looking questionable. What's strange is our hope still fixed on creative, high-paying work even as AI threatens to eliminate many jobs, including those. What's strange is the consequent doublespeak about leisure, and about the necessity of work that does not depend on college degrees. What's strange is our clumsiness in naming appreciation of human achievements except in terms of money.

---

15. Thistle, *From Marriage to the Market*, 47.
16. Hochschild and Machung, *Second Shift*; Boushey, *Finding Time*, 5–9.

BETTER THINKING ABOUT WORK

The work environment my childhood met seemed to solve problems people perennially confront. The future appeared to offer fun, high-paying jobs for men and women both rather than backbreaking struggle and housekeeping. Instead emphasis fell wrong in each category. Presumed fun and elective, work grew greedy and absorbed resources better spent elsewhere in life, though the market could not deliver all the cool jobs promised. If we imagine growing up as putting oneself into a job that bestows an identity and the income to live it out, in other words, as seeking one's fortune and getting a place to untie the cloth bundle from the stick, work will ask too much of us and we will ask too much of work. That paradigm errs on every count: that adulthood is attained by getting a job, that what we do for money is what makes us important.

When the tendency of an era is to worship work, we need a reminder that other places and times have prioritized leisure. Aristocracies the world over have insisted that some people should work and others should not, and in those systems people generally prefer to be in the second category. Though Americans have good reason to object to this division of labor, it is not obvious that enjoining labor for everybody is a victory. America has exemplars for bustlers and strivers, but not much usable past with models of leisure. Illustrious non-workers in America's past have compromising downsides, like those Tocqueville envisioned across the Ohio River, slaveholders whose blighting leisure came from the unpaid sweat of somebody else's brow. Even a perfect job, delivering the Goldilocks package of personal accomplishment and social benefit and ample cash, can be risky, not least by feeding the delusion that the worker is invincible or irreplaceable.

When the tendency of an era is to shirk work, different reminders are necessary. Post-COVID, more highly qualified people recognize that jobs may not deserve one's best self. Though some elite college students still flock to money-making careers and others bet on becoming influencers, others choose to prioritize stuff they love, like hobbies and friends. Historian Benjamin Kline Hunnicutt wishes workers would reclaim the "forgotten American dream" once cherished by our labor movements, seeking shorter hours rather than just full employment and more money. But young people constructing new models of work build them from the raw materials they were raised with, habituated to fun as end and ever-present means plus work as marker of worth. Demoting the work part of this equation leaves a lot of energy and time unaccounted for in an age when institutions and obligatory relationships have receded. What might be the implications of work's symbolic demotion for women, since work's symbolic importance for them was amplified by long confinement at home?[17]

Recognition of the limits long shaping women's work is reasonable start for rethinking work. Work will not disappear as long as we have bodies. Bodies need food, clothes, shelter, rest, healing, all of which depends on somebody's labor. The fact that many tasks in the past have been women's work gives women a certain standing to rethink the strangeness of American work. In their long exclusions from professions and their rewards, women developed art and craft in making things better for others. It is just that women now can test their capacities in many spheres, but it would be a pity to waste this long-acquired skill set. When work honors our bodily dependency and capacity to meet another's need, it can accommodate both the urgency of the jobs we do and their finitude. The market can wash our clothes and clean our toilets, but we really do want to receive from another labors of love. Much care work we expect and do for each other occurs because we actually care for each other. It is not possible to draw up the bill we have incurred by living and utterly impossible to pay it.

Ideas from Christian traditions can supply visions for work better than a fortune-seeking pig. This religious tradition supplies not one but many ideas about labor and rest. Christians might see work as creatively imitating what God does, participating or co-creating as befits creatures made in God's image. Or Christians might be troubled by work as burden, a finite means rather than holy end, with leisure our joy rather than work. Christians may cherish the Sabbath as regular rest and foretaste of heaven. The best-known Christian tradition regarding work comes from Reformation-era Protestants, who objected to excusing the priestly class from toil. Protestants proclaimed that God loved earnest labor when done in pursuit of one's vocation. Vocation means work to which one is summoned for the good of others and the glory of God. A vocation asks particular contribution of each, persons using their particular talents, "the place where our deep gladness meets the world's deep need," in Frederick Buechner's much-used definition. Misunderstandings notwithstanding, vocation is a great idea. To count as a vocation, work itself has to be worthy and serve the community. Both of those cut against American do-your-dream ideals. A calling is not to be whatever you want to be or to optimize your salary. Contract murder and drug dealing don't suffice. What makes the work good is

17. Hunnicutt, *Free Time*.

fidelity rather than quantity or market worth. If "what do you want to be when you grow up" is interpreted by American children to mean what job they want to hold, theology can offer other ways to answer the question: I want to be wise. I want to be a good human. I want to be a saint.[18]

Rejoicing to match one's skills to community need is a fine way to think about work. Regrettably, American pressures of productivity may too easily twist deep gladness and need into something that looks a lot like getting paid to do what one loves. More substantial correctives for work in our time might come from monasteries. St. Benedict of Nursia wrote a rule that put *ora* and *labora* together, prayer as a kind of work and work as a kind of prayer. Benedict assigned every member of a community a task, providing service to all and also to his or her own soul, imparting discipline and protecting from idleness. Workers should do their jobs without outsized pride in the product. Work should fit into the spaces around other important parts of life, like solitary reflection and communal prayer, the reception of guests, the fasting and feasting of the community, and the care of the earth and its creatures, rather than work squeezing other activities into its breaks or vacations.[19]

Taken together, monastic work, women's work, and the idea of vocation are good checks on American productivity culture. Kathleen Norris compares priestly work and women's work, likening a clergyman at Mass to "a kind of daft housewife" whose enactment of holy rites resembles the mealtime puttering a woman would do in a kitchen. The work that monks lay aside day by day, like the housework women traditionally have done, gets taken up and laid aside daily, never really done because finishing is not the point. We are all finite and embodied and eat and sleep every day, which means we have to keep doing the work, but also that we are free to put it down when something else wants us. Work can be a glorious way to harmonize body, mind, and soul, making the work of our hands serve aspirations of hearts. More could be said of work. But work might be served better by saying less.[20]

---

18. Meilaender, ed., *Working*; Pieper, *Leisure the Basis of Culture*; Buechner, *Wishful Thinking*, 119.

19. Malesic, "'Nothing Is to Be Preferred,'" 45–61.

20. Norris, *Quotidian Mysteries*, 3.

Chapter 4

Friends and Lovers (Marriage)

THERE'S A MOMENT IN the musical *Fiddler on the Roof* when Tevye's daughters, who have been hoping the matchmaker will pick husbands for them, dancing blithely while hanging laundry and swirling around the garden, understand marriage might be something to dread. Even the rich or handsome man of their dreams would claim their obedience, bodily service, and pains on the path to motherhood, and if a man brought by the matchmaker were poor or cruel they would still owe those things. The character Tevye is a poor Jewish milkman whose domestic life plays out against the backdrop of pogrom-ridden Russia and changing mores, themes that partly explain why the Broadway musical (1964) and film (1971) were popular among Cold War viewers in their own seasons of bewilderment. When Tevye, echoing his daughters' aspirations for love, asks his wife if she loves him, she instead lists her daily acts of service for twenty-five years, cooking and cleaning and raising children. Eventually both characters admit it's nice to know they love each other. Work may be love made plain, but love is still nice to know. I used to think this play was about antisemitism and family life in the clash of tradition and modernity. But then neighborliness put me and my young children in the front row of a performance that cast my neighbor's son, a middle schooler with white-blonde hair, as Tevye, and I had to explain to my kids why the daughters wanted a match. Each of Tevye's daughters wants someone handsome and desirable, a catch, to choose her. Then it occurs to them that married life is not just romance and cozy homemaking but appetites and offspring, chores and subordination and aging. Tevye's daughters beg the matchmaker not to rush The daughters' voices and expressions change. Sung by middle-school girls, the spectacle is altogether weep-worthy.[1]

Weddings wrap up marriage in an enticing package. Is the wedding a party for the bride, the spoonful of sugar to chase bitter medicine because otherwise no woman would take it willingly? Does the bride's celebration demonstrate that marriage really is about love, or the opposite? It would be foolish to offer one explanation for everybody's marital conditions. But explaining why American culture around marriage has turned out to be so strange is useful to orient anyone navigating it to find or keep a spouse.

A SHORT HISTORY OF AMERICAN MARRIAGE

The prehistory is long. God made marriage in the beginning, a natural institution. Because it was not good for the human to be alone, God made a helper so thereafter man would leave his parents and be united to his wife (Gen 2:18, 24). What God put together humans were not supposed to take apart (Mark 10:6–9). Greeks had ideals of marital union too, Plato's *Symposium* describing people's quest for soulmates, for the perfect other half to restore the wholeness they had before Zeus sundered it. Romantic love in recognizable form rose out of the mists of the Middle Ages, a different beast from the married kind. The former was courtly, prizing unattainable or unrequited or unconsummated love, brimming with longing and admiration. The latter bred offspring and sorted property.[2]

American marital history might be described, historian Stephanie Coontz suggests, as a story about how love conquered marriage. According to that view, the evolution of marriage goes like this. Marriage used to prioritize legal and financial arrangements. Families traded property, counted children as legal heirs, and placed men and women into standard roles. It was possible that couples might enjoy parts of the traditional arrangement but enjoyment was not the point. Enjoyment became the point with the advent of companionate marriage, which arose in the 1700s or the 1800s or the 1920s, depending on who tells this chapter of the story, when men and women started choosing each other for a life together, not so much to honor law or custom but because they liked each other.[3]

---

1. Jewison, dir., *Fiddler on the Roof*.
2. Kass and Kass, eds., *Wing to Wing*, 1–18, 86, 215–31, 244.
3. Coontz, *Marriage*.

Friends and Lovers (Marriage)

The Protestant character of the United States is partly responsible for the centrality of marriage in public life. Christianity governed and shaped marriage over centuries. Jesus blessed the wedding at Cana with a miracle (John 2:1–11) and advised that the resurrected would neither marry nor be given in marriage (Matt 22:30). Marriage is the way Scripture describes Christ's relationship to his people, the church as beloved bride of Christ (Eph 5:25–32, Rev 19:7). The disciples of Jesus understood marriage as a worthy if not ultimate estate. Paul approved marriage but preferred singleness. From those principles, Roman Catholics extrapolated canon law around marriage and clerical institutions elevating celibacy. Rejecting consecrated celibacy, in the sixteenth century Martin Luther and colleagues elevated marriage. To their credit, early Protestants reckoned seriously with the fact of the body, that its appetites rendered celibacy a promise nearly impossible to keep, which made sin and guilt hard to bear. They reasoned with sound scriptural warrant that it is better to marry than to burn (1 Cor 7:9). Protestants' elimination of consecrated celibacy implied that marriage was for everybody, the one legitimate path in adulthood. Legal historian John Witte explains the transition of marriage to a civil estate, a matter of contract rather than sacrament. In the Anglo-American realm the institution also was framed as intimate covenant relationship or the founding of a little commonwealth.[4]

Marriage functioned as gateway and framework to adult life and citizenship through the first centuries of the new nation. When he visited the United States to size up its customs, Alexis de Tocqueville noticed how much Americans valued marriage. He also noticed that for women, marriage was a comparatively bad deal. American girls were more free than European ones and had more choice about husbands. Once girls consented, though, the wife's subordination to the husband held fast.[5]

A wife's role in nineteenth-century America was framed by coverture, an idea borrowed from English law, marking her as a person represented or covered in public by her husband, the woman implicitly included in the man's exercise of citizenship. On those grounds states commonly prevented married women from voting, owning property, receiving their own wages, and testifying in court. Custody of children defaulted to fathers. Women's rights movements pressed to reverse these injustices. The beautiful suffragist and abolitionist Lucy Stone kept turning down the marriage proposals

---

4. Witte, *From Sacrament to Contract*, 2–11.
5. Tocqueville, *Democracy in America*, 686–89; Dabling, *New Birth of Marriage*.

of Henry Blackwell, scion of one of America's most prominent reform families. She liked *him* well enough but she could not stand what American marriage was. When they finally wed, Stone wrote protest vows, making clear that she and Henry were consenting to the choice of each other but not to the legal arrangement offered to them.[6]

In the United States, marriage is a creature of the state, first a civil thing rather than a churchly one. Though many couples marry in church, even still, the state license is the part that counts. Individual states, not the national government, control most features of marriage. Variations appeared across states and across racial groups through the nineteenth century. Before the Civil War, some states forbade enslaved people to marry and some after the war forbade interracial marriage. Major Supreme Court decisions like the 1967 *Loving v. Virginia*, invalidating laws against interracial marriage, and the 2005 decision *Obergefell v. Hodges*, upholding same-sex marriage, wrought change nationwide, at once reflecting and redirecting culture.[7]

Nineteenth-century Americans understood marriage as key to shaping adulthood for men and women both, but not in the same way. Men's and women's separate spheres had relational and economic consequences. Industrialization drew sharper lines around a household economy that configured the domestic sphere as the female domain. For men, marriage might denote status and provide comfort. For women it was basically a job. As Charlotte Perkins Gilman pressed the question, "The girl must marry: else how live?" The contract was supposed to work this way, in Gilman's assessment. Women would exchange sex and housework for financial support, with love as the bait or the glue or the window dressing to what was fundamentally an economic proposition. Since single women had questionable standing in the public realm and were barred from many kinds of employment, middle-class women could not easily support themselves. Therefore, the supposition held that they entered marriage not just for the sake of a relationship but vocationally.[8]

Twentieth-century arrangements changed swiftly, offering both men and women new roles. America's first sexual revolution happened in the 1920s. Divorce rates crept up, worrying experts. In that decade, Colorado

---

6. McMillen, *Lucy Stone*, 128.

7. Cott, *Public Vows*; Mintz, *Prime of Life*, 102–8.

8. Hartog, *Man and Wife in America*; Mintz, *Prime of Life*, 102–10, 120–25; Gilman, *Women and Economics*, quoted in Wallace, *All Dressed in White*, 13.

judge Ben Lindsey proposed companionate marriage, a bond dissolvable if no children were involved. Off and on in preceding several centuries, advice writers had bidden men and women to develop the affective side of their life together, the part devoted to conversation and games and garden strolls. This newer companionate marriage aimed to unite what the Middle Ages had kept apart, romantic love and the household kind. Twentieth-century models acknowledged that husbands and wives maybe had less need of each other's labors and thus needed more to do together to fill the space between grunts of bed, board, and barn. In the 1930s and 1940s, new manners also afforded more opportunity for male-female fun on the way to marriage. Dating relocated from front porch to the back seat, historian Beth Bailey explains. Marriage ages dipped younger in the 1950s, with men back from battlefields and middle-class couples offered postwar promises of fulfillment at home.[9]

By the 1960s the generation raised around mid-century happy hearths gagged on all that domestic felicity, preferring almost any arrangement to wedding bells and white picket fences. Free love and shacking up went live in the 1970s, though they did not become ordinary overnight. Plenty of men and women across all demographics still met and married and had kids. But norms were changing profoundly. Feminism altered gender roles and consequently spousal ones. American Christians trying to respond to the sexual revolution domesticated some of its innovations. When its lure tempted the godly, Christian advice-writers tried to reinforce fidelity by making it sexy. To keep men from straying, Marabel Morgan advised wives that the complementary combination of seductiveness and submission would keep them irresistible to husbands. A sign of a time in transition: the late-1960s TV show *I Dream of Jeannie*, whose reruns I watched after school, revolves around the antics of a blonde-ponytailed woman named Jeannie who walks around in a bikini top and gauze pants and does magic and lives with her sort-of boyfriend, an Air Force pilot, without being married. But also Jeannie, who really is a genie, calls him "Master" and whenever she crosses him he orders her to get back into her bottle, which he can cork, and all she really wants is for him to make her his wife so she can dress up and cook him dinner to eat by candlelight.[10]

It was a confusing time.

9. Bailey, *From Front Porch to Back Seat*; Mintz, *Prime of Life*, 120.
10. Syfers, "I Want a Wife"; Morgan, *Total Woman*, 38; Celello, *Making Marriage Work*.

Times would get more confusing still as the familiar parts of love stories got selectively remade while once-transgressive behaviors were becoming normal. What went wrong with dating and marriage was not only the reduced ability to live up to norms but demolition of the norms themselves. Norms broken are hard to repair. The institution of marriage was buffeted from all sides, people choosing it later, ending it earlier, or not marrying at all. By the early twenty-first century, more Americans were spending less of their adult lives married. Young adults launched into early adulthood paired and maybe living together for a period, maybe to marry, maybe not.[11]

In a related development, girls and boys also learned how to be friends. Announcing this new possibility, the 1989 film *When Harry Met Sally* proposed to audiences that men and women could not be friends because, as the character Harry kept insisting, sex would always get in the way. Friendship would founder on physical attraction. But men and women had better learn to be friends, because companionship increasingly seemed like the chief reason why American middle-class couples wanted to marry. After all, even Aristotle thought that men and women *could* be friends if they had similar education and pursuits, which men and women did not in ancient Greece but could in the United States in the 1990s. The film's plot resolves the conundrum by showing a successful opposite-sex friendship followed by the happy promise of becoming husband and wife, the friends wildly in love, sex getting in the best way. That was the era's reigning ideal and not just for romantic comedy.[12]

Imagining male-female friendship in the abstract may have been startling in the 1990s. But praise for marital friendship was not new. Nineteenth- and twentieth-century writers hoped sexual equality would reshape marriage to foster this friendship. John Stuart Mill (1806–1873) saw marriage ideally as a partnership of bright people entering a contract as equals, such that children and even sex figured less significantly than enjoyment of each other's refined companionship. Simone de Beauvoir (1908–1986) conceived of marriage as two "entirely self-sufficient human beings" drawn together by friendship that did not interrupt their work or other relationships, a couple at once lovers and friends who did not "seek in each other

---

11. Mintz, *Prime of Life*, 98, 102–3; Horowitz, Graf, and Livingston, "Marriage and Cohabitation Rates"; Manning, Brown, and Payne, "Two Decades of Stability"; Fukuyama, *Great Disruption*.

12. Reiner, dir., *When Harry Met Sally*.

their sole reasons for living." The new normalcy of late twentieth-century male-female friendships made this kind of marriage more accessible. The stock line of 1990s self-scripted wedding vows, perhaps more successfully authentic than eloquent, was, "Today, I marry my best friend."[13]

Harry and Sally's problem would seem quaint long before the twenty-first century aged to double digits. Of course men and women could be friends. Whatever anxiety male-female friendships once might have caused were neutralized not because Harry was wrong in the first place but because both desire and friendship could be channeled elsewhere. Broader acceptance came for same-sex coupling and for sexual activity disconnected from romance. Friends could exchange sexual favors, renamed benefits. The prevalence of no-strings-attached sex might even have seemed useful to safeguard male-female friendships. The freer engagements of boys and girls, men and women, veered off in many directions and spiraled away from marriage. Sex turned out to be no big deal, but also like candy, and also urgent and ubiquitous. Dating apps promoted broader and briefer sexual contacts, Tinder and other platforms enabling gratification without delay. College students, including those on Christian campuses, got good at resolutely steeling themselves with alcohol before weekends' sexual conquests. Young adults trained in those environments learned to take up contacts often depersonalized and transitory. Christine Emba finds women less than content with this system but playing along lest they lose romantic prospects altogether. Men and women both report social isolation and loneliness.[14]

The twenty-first-century path from meeting to marriage became less clearly marked than in the past. Shifts in dating encouraged wandering off-path before reaching the finish line. The finish line changed too, marriage less often presupposed permanent. For some, especially less affluent couples, marriage came to serve as capstone late in adulthood rather than cornerstone at its start. Andrew Cherlin calls America's unique and problematic patterns of coupling the "marriage-go-round," our individualism making citizens more likely to start as well as end marriages than others in socioeconomically similar countries. From the 1960s to the 1980s, divorce rates rose, with a sharp uptick following legal turns to no-fault laws. The Uniform Marriage and Divorce Act (UMDA) in the 1970s guided states on dissolving marriages and managing the consequences, like alimony,

---

13. Mill and de Beauvoir treated in Yenor, *Family Politics*, 128–29, 189; Mendelson, *Vows*; Witte, *From Sacrament to Contract*, 200–202.

14. Beste, *College Hookup Culture*; Emba, *Rethinking Sex*.

custody, and property division. By the 1980s popular opinion took for granted that half of marriages ended in divorce. Do half of marriages end in divorce? Not quite, because the rates are not the same across economic brackets. Divorce rates dropped a bit in the early twenty-first century. Marriage became a class marker. Unions of people with college education and at least moderate wealth still hold up pretty well. Relationships of poorer couples are less likely to turn into marriage, and if they do, are likelier to end in divorce.[15]

MARRIAGE IN LIVED EXPERIENCE

Every Saturday was wedding day across the street from Baba's house in the summer. When cars lined up on the street and it wasn't the regular Mass time or a funeral, somebody was getting married at St. Mary's. I watched the guests going in the front, and an hour or so later I watched the bride, having been made a Mrs., make her grand exit down the stairs at the back of the church. Brides always wore big white dresses. They had veils attached to little crowns on top of their heads. Bridesmaids wore matching dresses, mauve or teal or plum. The people standing in receiving lines down St. Mary's back stairs looked basically like my mother's wedding pictures, because that was what weddings looked like.

My grandmother did not look like that when she got married. That was not the custom of people in her social situation when she married in 1930. Lively daughter of respected worker and farmer, my grandmother was a catch. She did not change her name when she got married because she and my grandfather already had the same last name. They were distant cousins.

My parents married in 1960. The Pittsburgh Pirates won the pennant that year, which made traffic crazy when my mother was driving to the store in the Strip district to pick up her dress. That wholesale neighborhood had dresses she could afford, which made it possible to get married in a big white dress. The autumn she got married, she was living in an upstairs bedroom in her parents' house, still taking the cross-town bus to finish up her last semester at Duquesne. Because she had class on Saturdays, she had to ask her English professor to excuse her that day. He was reluctant. What for?, he asked. She told him she was going to a wedding. Whose?, he asked,

---

15. Cherlin, *Marriage-Go-Round*, 138; Andersen and Scherer, "US Marriage and Divorce."

Friends and Lovers (Marriage)

still reluctant, whose wedding are you missing my class to attend? Mine! She exclaimed with triumph.

Triumphant my mother looks in the best picture in their wedding album, she holding her hoop skirt up a few inches to clear the curb as she tiptoes across the street from her parents' house to the church. Her big white dress has tiers of ruffles. Her bridesmaids are dressed in olive green and gold. My mother looks gleeful in her wedding pictures. No one has any idea what is coming. The first time I saw this picture was in my father's office on a visit once. I found the albums in a box in the corner. Until then I had not known that pictures of their wedding existed. By family reports, my parents' marriage was fine until after my younger brother was born. My father was a grad student working in a lab then. My mother insists that they were happy until radiation from lab experiments did something. I did not observe the change, only what happened after.

How to introduce my father? He should be better known. By me, for starters, except getting to know him seemed repugnant as long as he lived so I did not do it, which I regret. I recognize with considerable reluctance that he should have introduction here. He was the late-born son of a Slovak railroad worker from the same Pennsylvania-Ohio world as my mother. He served in the army, had a doctorate in chemistry, ran for elective office. After divorce he resisted paying child support because he charged that he was the injured party, and if the state were going to give custody to my mother then the state could support our rearing. I have memories of a few times with him, most not good. Dwelling on them tempts uncharity. My siblings and I turned out okay. Time went on, healing happened, people helped. But lives were built over a layer prone to rot, crack, leak, fumes. Lifelong since we are taken by surprise in moments when the scrim fails, cracked plank over flood creek, crumbling cellar wall, yellow-green ooze out of overfull diaper, and we have to figure out in panic how to paste things together with the other resources the good parts of time since have stocked. Repair can't always be done cleanly and is always a labor and it needs doing sometimes when neither time nor labor permits. I missed my chance to reckon with my father in person because I spent too long declaring him irrelevant. I regret that.

In my 1970s childhood I learned most about marriage from two sources: *The Bride Game* and the DSWC picnic.

That everyone wanted to grow up to be married was a given, to me obvious in the breach. How one would get there, and what being married would be like for the rest of life, that was unclear. Sometimes social critics contemn girls of ages past for all the emotional energy they loaded into weddings, rueful that their hopes and ambitions had to be crimped to fit into the narrow shell of wife. I don't much blame those girls, not when there were few other realms on offer for their hopes and ambitions and none costumed so well. I did not obsess about weddings and assumed there was lots more to life. But still, a wedding could be fine or tacky. The wedding a person could make the way she wanted, once she got a prospective groom to initiate the process, and so a person should learn to want the best things she could get. That I learned from *The Bride Game*.

Our Pittsburgh cousins had a closet full of board games and our family's five kids made playing them more interesting. Sometimes we played *The Game of Life*, where competitors in plastic sedans set out to seek their fortunes, getting a college degree, starting a family, taking a job and a mortgage, the part of the game none of us understood. Luck determined a lot. Strong starts usually predetermined victory. Still, the choice of paths was up to each player and there were a lot of us. In contrast, only the girl cousins were allowed to play *The Bride Game*, whose object was to collect cards showing a rightly attired wedding party (Evening Formal, Daytime Formal, Daytime Semiformal, or Daytime Informal), plus cards for something old, something new, something borrowed, and something blue, plus a cake, bouquet, and jewelry. When a player had a matched bridal party and accessories, she rolled again to advance down the aisle. The winner was the one who made it to the end of the aisle with all her matching stuff first. What happened next? What happened after the descent from St. Mary's stairs under hail of well-wishing rice? In bridal magazines, we saw heart-shaped bathtubs in Poconos hotels. There were no cards for that in *The Bride Game*.

The first three sets of nuptial garments in *The Bride Game* box looked nearly indistinguishable to us. Bridal gowns in all three fancy card sets—Evening Formal, Daytime Formal, Daytime Semiformal—were long with veils and trains. We knew Evening was the most luxe and the rest came in descending order, but nuances of the black-tie or white-tie dress code were lost on us. That was not our world. All three of these card sets looked the way brides look. The exception was the Daytime Informal. The Daytime Informal dress was not even a gown. Daytime Informal was ugly. We were no more willing to win the game with the Daytime Informal groom than we would be willing ourselves to be the Daytime Informal bride, with her knee-length yellow dress and a stupid floppy hat instead of crown and veil.

Friends and Lovers (Marriage)

Settling for the Daytime Informal would mean conceding that *that* was who I am, all I deserve. Of course the game manufacturers were trying to be relevant. Of course they intended for players to take these choices personally, as we did. Not that the game accommodated all the different girls who might be playing. There was no racial diversity in the stack of brides and grooms. There was no one in the game who looked like me either. My cousins and I could want Evening Formal in the same way we might want to be princesses, but we were not the kind of people whose weddings would actually look like any of these. We were the kind of people who had stuffed cabbage and kielbasa at our wedding receptions, and polkas and dollar dances.

Big families have lots of weddings. I went to many as a kid, including some we were invited to. Most of the weddings we attended as actual guests blend together, lighting up a corridor of western Pennsylvania and eastern Ohio. The wedding Mass was mostly the same with occasional adjustments to the liturgy. Some couples lighted a unity candle or, in the 1980s, carried bottles of sand to the altar to mix together to symbolize blending of bride's and groom's lives never to be sifted apart again. Receptions happened downstairs in church halls full of food and people, aunts laying tables with roaster pans of cabbage and noodles, sausage and peppers, potato dumplings. Pittsburgh wedding receptions had cookie tables with nut horns, pineapple squares, and pizzelles. Adults found the bar and children sat at big tables and drank lemonade. There would be a dollar dance, when my mother or aunt might give me a dollar to put in the cigar box of a man standing next to the bride, who would put her hands on the shoulders of each person in line and sway for a few minutes in payment. The brides always looked gorgeous to me. Their dresses were consistently a working-class version of the big white dress, approximately Daytime Semiformal. At some point late in the reception, the groom threw a garter. Then the bride threw a bouquet. People went home happy and tipsy.

From the game and these weddings, I assumed the following about marriage. Getting married meant having someone choose you. It meant having a big party where the bride got to select all the best stuff, as prize for having been picked and as an expression of her good taste. Marriage meant something having to do with sex, a fact both categorical and obscure. For women even a few decades earlier marriage was rigid expectation, and for women a few decades later all of this was up for grabs. I grew up thinking getting married was normal whether or not it actually still was.

One wedding in the Pennsylvania-Ohio circuit stands out. My mother drove from Pittsburgh to take my grandmother to a cousin's daughter's wedding and they made me come along. We got there late, barely seated before the bride was walked to the altar not by her father as is traditional but by both parents, all three rosy from the farm, old-school family trying out modern ways, three arm-in-arm wearing stout Sunday best and not quite fitting through the narrow aisle. With each jerky step one edged forward to make room for the other two to squeeze up behind, which made me laugh, which made my mother laugh, shaking and in tears, which made my grandmother mad. She gave my mother a sharp elbow and told her to keep quiet. At the reception hall, the buffet had matching gelatin molds in the shape of the bride and groom's initials, one clear gelatin and the other creamy. For the garter toss, the couple expanded the ritual into something like a game show. The groom's friends manacled the couple to chairs with a ball and chain and made the bride and groom promise each other things like this: Groom, do you promise to put the toilet seat down, I do; Bride, do you promise not to take beers out of the fridge to fit in a gallon of milk, I do; Groom, do you promise not to complain when we go to dinner at my mother's, I do. The older people did not like this game. Neither my mother nor my grandmother laughed. This garter ceremony lifted the lid a little too much from the marital package to show what lay inside. Even silly weddings added something to my sense that marriage was good.

I knew divorce was bad. Our household's divorce was so bad that I mistook it for the way divorces just were as a category. What I took as typical for divorce were the times when my father would come back to town to celebrate one of our birthdays and we climbed into his car, Daddy! Daddy!, and he took us out to Howard Johnsons and we ate fried clam strips. My mother was not invited to these dinners so she came later to pick us up in the parking lot at HoJo's, which had exceptionally good chocolate ice cream, and shuttled us into the back seat as quickly as she could while he cursed her out as a dirty rotten something something something who took his children away from him. I'm sure being divorced meant many things to my mother that were lost on me. The scarcity of divorced people among families we knew could be read as proof of a healthy community, though at the time what I noticed more was that we maybe had a taint that other people did not. Understandably, my mother wanted the fellowship of other people in the same boat she found herself.

Friends and Lovers (Marriage)

For that reason, I should have been more understanding when she joined the Divorced, Separated, and Widowed Catholics (DSWC) group. The DSWC was way beyond my understanding. I hardly understood what divorce was. It was inconceivable to me that a number of other people sufficiently large to put together a club was also going through the same violence we were. Furthermore, the name of the group puzzled me. On the one hand, I knew few other people whose parents were divorced. So maybe the group had to branch out or else there wouldn't be enough guests for a picnic. On the other hand, when I eventually met people with divorced parents, their arrangements were so different they hardly merited the same terminology. Divorced people who showed up together at little league games and sat in the same row of the bleachers, who were these people? Why did they bother to get divorced, if the ex-husband didn't scream at the ex-wife and drive off to live somewhere else and make fear seep like poison gas underneath the apartment door when he arrived? Like, why even bother?

The remarkable thing, looking back, is how much the DSWC insisted on all three categories in welcoming members to its group. It was not a single parents group. These people weren't singles. They would be married if they could. They had not stopped being Catholic either or believing in God. God invented marriage. God intended loving union for these people who had gotten roughed up by the world. Still, I thought there had to be a lot of difference between being divorced, separated, or widowed. I knew what the shame was of the first word even if not everybody's divorces were equally terrible. Separated maybe could be turned around. Widowhood happened when somebody died. That was sad but there was no shame in it.

DSWC picnics were not only for divorced, separated, and widowed adults, but for the kids they dragged along to get to know each other in a comfortable social environment. The picnics tried to solve the problem I admitted was a problem, that often I felt like the only kid with divorced parents. Still, what I had in common with those other kids at the picnics I could not figure out. At the picnics I stood around waiting in line for a dry hockey-puck hamburger or burnt hot dog, wondering what was supposed to happen. Part of the problem was my incompetence at the games kids play at state parks: softball, volleyball, freeze tag, hide and seek. But probably there was no way of making those gatherings fun. My siblings and I hung around awkwardly and hoped there would be some good dessert, mostly sticking together with our backs to other people until it was time to get in the car and leave. We knew enough children of DSWC parents by just knowing each other.

Thanks be to God for the DSWC picnics, for the mosquitoes and the well-done meat and the store-bought pie, because they granted me a pass to skip most of the transformations that American culture wrought on dating and marriage in the next decades except for the divorce-related ones that hit us early. Kids from DSWC picnics mostly didn't dream of free love or cohabitation or polyamory. We wanted the thing we didn't have, the normal household, the parents who kissed each other. That plus my mousy nerdiness plus my demographic cohort just shy of the invention of dating apps protected me from most of the other later transformations. Not until decades later did popular culture tell girls that "smart is the new pretty," a useless nostrum even were it true, replaced soon after by strong as the new pretty, both revisions hard to take seriously as long as all attributes still get judged by the measure of pretty.

With new opportunities opened for women, I was encouraged to think that it fell to me to choose a future I would prefer and that it was up to someone else to choose me, whereupon I would integrate myself into his plans. If there was a contradiction in those ideas, I did not see it. When it was time to for me to acquire something old, something new, something borrowed, and something blue for real, and then step my way up the aisle, I married a southerner. My sister made my dress. I wore a thing on my head similar to a crown with a short veil. It all looked lovely. No one wore floppy hats. When I returned from my honeymoon with a changed name, some graduate-school colleagues made a show of their inability to locate my office mailbox because they said my name wasn't there any more, by which they meant my old name (they would not have said maiden name), signaling their disapproval.

The Bride Game taught me that I would be guest of honor at a gala that the big good of marriage deserved. DSWC picnics taught me that living a marriage was harder than planning a wedding, but still a big good. There was a lot that neither phenomenon taught me. Maybe it would have been better to walk into marriage clear-eyed and sober, as in the Eastern Orthodox liturgy that places crowns on heads of both bride and groom, marking the kingdom of heaven and also their mutual martyrdom. That was not the reason ever given to me for the crown-like headpieces on veils. I have heard men joke about their wives as the old ball and chain, and worry that the good-looking women they married would "let themselves go." The first time I attended a high-school reunion I got seated next to a woman who told me she had four elective C-sections because she wanted to keep herself up for her husband. Weddings were pretty but, as the Ohio couple with matching gelatin molds let slip, some things about marriage might not be.

WHAT'S STRANGE ABOUT PURSUING MARRIAGE THIS WAY

More surprising than changes to marriage is its strange persistence as an ideal. Moralists rail against hookup culture and divorce rates, but the real question is why young men and women, with infinite coupling options, continue to marry at all. If love conquered marriage, why doesn't the vanquished creature just die already? American society might have scrapped marriage in favor of other domestic arrangements. polycules or civil unions or temporary commitments with renewable contracts. At large in erotic social life, consent overrules and substitutes for most other rules formerly applied to pairings. When sex was cut free from marriage and babies or from any relationship whatsoever, cut free even from most constraints of embodiment like time and space, and sex is putatively what people want, why saddle oneself with anything else?[16]

Some women, outliers weaponizing affected domesticity as counterculture, double down on the trappings of the old social institution, playing tradwife for the camera. One might have guessed that the girl should not marry at all now that she could live perfectly well on her own. To some girls, the deal marriage used to offer—bread and board in exchange for sex, children, and housework—had begun long ago to look shabby in contrast to the other things she could choose. The things women had previously gotten through marriage could be gotten other ways, given or taken otherwise and without commitment. To be sure, plenty of women with means and desire to avoid marriage now do avoid it. Rather than liberate themselves from the whole thing, though, many American women have kept on wanting the engagement and the vows and the party and the spouse.[17]

Women might have decided just to live with partners rather than getting caught up in consumerist fantasies of weddings. Instead, for decades many have kept choosing big weddings, insisting on and paying for big weddings. In the past, the big fact of marriage justified the big outlay of

---

16. Brake, ed., *After Marriage*.
17. Traister, *All the Single Ladies*.

weddings. All that the couple was bringing together forever, plus the social approval to their sexual union, were reasons sufficient to make large claims on families and communities for travel and feasting and gifts. For brides, to the extent that weddings were especially *their* party, the point of the sparkly trappings was sweetening the deal as they entered an estate that, though good, could be hard. If massive wedding parties used to be justified as proportionate according to the significance of the event, the new style of marriage might have downsized the old party.

The scale of weddings in late twentieth- and early twenty-first centuries promised parties in the old-fashioned style in service of a renovated institution. Some couples might consider that renovation itself cause for the huge celebration. From the outside, marriage for a twenty-first-century young adult might look like the stodgy cramped thing one's parents lived in. But, like the process of remodeling a dumpy house on scarce real estate in a good neighborhood, the renovated model of marriage bought access to a bunch of desirable features once it was stripped of negatives that previously seemed to make it unlivable.

Marriage could be made very livable indeed. Because many women still want to marry and can marry in ways that appear to deliver benefits without the problems feminists lambasted fifty years ago, they have every incentive to do up their weddings. It really *is* their day. Brides not only have made over the wedding day but the happily-ever-after part. No one really likes divorce—who would, if you could avoid it?—but women in new social situations want marriage that suits who they are and what they want. They can avoid old stereotypes around *wife* and *husband*, in part through nongendered designations for that other person, like spouse (good old word from the Latin for betrothal) or partner (not so good a word, irredeemably associated with contracts and business). In past periods, women sometimes had to cede personal ambitions to get a husband, but increasingly women's higher ambitions yield better husbands. For less affluent and less educated men and women, a marriage and a wedding have become things to do later, if at all, when money was saved to pay for them.[18]

Weddings in the late twentieth century got gigantic. Expectations and budgets ballooned. Parties grew even more glitzy and gimmicky once the invention of social media upped the ante. Luxuries billed as traditions turned mandatory: big dress, big veil, overflowing flowers, formal invitations, full court of attendants, fine food, lavish bar, trendy cake, party favors.

---

18. Jellison, *It's Our Day*, 60–62; Dunak, *As Long as We Both Shall Love*.

FRIENDS AND LOVERS (MARRIAGE)

Brides' white dresses stayed big in scale and on the bottom—floor-length skirt, train, tucks, pleats, tulle—while reducing on top, ubiquitous strapless dresses epitomizing early twenty-first-century style, a nod to tradition with a sexy wink. The huge weddings of the period were at once more public events and more individualized ones, celebrating the couple's appreciation of their own reciprocal dazzlement more than a union of families. Couples could take advantage of new state licensing rules to draft parents or friends or coaches to officiate, personalizing the ceremony even further. Weddings became the couple's party, mostly the bride's.[19]

Why did weddings get bigger just when marriage was shrinking in social significance? By the late twentieth century, all components of married life were accessible without marriage: public-facing monogamy, shared residence, parenthood. Once conventional rationales for wedding details were evacuated, those flourishes were ready for retirement. Reality drained significance from symbolic stuff at weddings, which called forth ever more stuff to be piled on to elevate festivities. Markets were happy to cooperate, selling nearly infinite accessories to make a bride's day more special and unique and just like what all the other brides are doing, also in faint imitation of televised weddings of English princesses. Sometimes this seems fun. Who wants to scrimp on their special day? But disproportions of expense and pomp in weddings came to weigh on couples themselves. Though 2020s trends unsurprisingly tamp down wedding excess, smaller, sometimes quirkier "non-wedding" weddings differ from budget-busting blow-outs in degree not kind, prioritizing the couple's tastes and pleasures, besting other brides and grooms in novelty rather than just expense. Sometimes now couples decide to get the actual wedding over with right away, scheduling weddings even before, say, the rehearsal dinner at start of a full weekend's activities, to put the most stressful part behind and get on with the fun. Also some couples schedule honeymoons before weddings, the pair's gift to themselves to compensate for the stress of planning the big day. Newer status markers if not necessarily smaller budgets updated weddings' brand of individualistic luxury.[20]

That weddings got bigger as a ritual in adulthood enabled inclusion of those who had felt sidelined or oppressed by the institution in earlier eras. The legal success of same-sex marriage reflected and amplified, at least

---

19. Jellison, *It's Our Day*, 6; Rebecca Mead studies the commercial success of "Inventing the Traditionalesque" in *One Perfect Day*, 55–74.
20. Krueger, "First Comes Marriage."

temporarily, the ideal of marriage as socially favored form for a permanent loving union in the United States. Some same-sex couples embraced the institution rather than rejecting it as oppressive or using their love to contemn or explode it. Indeed, in popular imagination same-sex couples embraced the institution so effectively that Stephanie Coontz in 2020 wrote that most American couples wish their marriages were "gayer," two desirable people living together enjoyably as equals beyond old-fashioned gender roles.[21]

The big wedding party has come to communicate so much about a sense of self that some women have hosted weddings while declaring independence from spouses or relationships. These women hold ceremonies to marry themselves, hosting their own I-choose-myself party to celebrate their satisfaction. Sologamy declares to others that a woman does not need to wait around for somebody to choose her, a match, but is fully content alone, herself her own catch. Marrying yourself may seem silly, but it is not that strange in a period where self-fulfillment is made the point of marriage.

What's strange about the way Americans marry is that they still do it at all, having dissolved most reasons and social supports for doing it. What's strange about weddings is that they keep happening, ever more elaborate and often abstracted from the union they aim to adorn. What's strange is the old mismatch between floral glorious wedding celebrations and the ball-and-chain lives people face, reset for contemporary realities. What's strange is that Americans lament loneliness and disconnection while maximizing choices and minimizing obligation.

BETTER THINKING ABOUT MARRIAGE

The models of love and marriage my childhood met seemed to solve many problems people perennially confront. Getting to be together with one's heart's desire, friend and dream date and fellow adventurer all in one, is a better way for paired adulthood than arranged spouse and property consolidation. It is better for women than subordination and drudgery. In fact that package is so good it can expand broadly outward, embracing children, neighbors, older relations, community. Instead emphasis fell wrong in each category. Sex beat out romance and permanence rather than making married life fun from this day forward. Marriage got priced out of reach for Americans who could not afford permanent monogamy.

---

21. Eskridge Jr. and Riano, *Marriage Equality*; Coontz, "Make Your Marriage Gayer."

Friends and Lovers (Marriage)

At the very least, history offers suggestive contrasts demonstrating that the way we love does not inevitably have to take this shape. Some ways of dating and mating in the past were worse. What looks necessary by current fashions actually is not. One does not have to do this. Some stupidities one can opt out of right away. Delete Tinder profile, don't do the Nashville bachelorette party, don't take a honeymoon before a wedding, and so forth. History also may help reclaim boundaries when everything appears to be up for grabs.

Particularly discouraging are historical contrasts on this side of sexual liberations that promised to remove impediments imposed on true love by law, prudery, morality, bigotry, or piety. The revolutions that happened since my *Bride Game* days promised satisfaction, equality, toleration, harmony. Observation suggests many people get no such satisfaction. As weddings demonstrate, love and marriage may seem like incredibly personal and unique phenomena but are always social in reciprocal ways. One's private relationship is others' business, not least because couples seek others' acceptance and celebration. Social expectations teach men and women what to want, what to put up with, what to hold out for.

Norms about dating and marriage dismantled a half-century or so ago neither have been rebuilt nor replaced coherently, so the landscape a person must traverse when trying to find love and grow in it is a pockmarked minefield. COVID rendered explorations of eros even more risky and awkward than usual—New York public health guidelines in 2020 advising partners to avoid breathing on each other during sex, for example—though the pandemic's aftermath may have redoubled desires for connection. The systems through which men and women meet have disaggregated the components of embodied connection while trying to name fleetingly the thing that each party, owing each other nothing more than consent, hopes to get. Young people display breathtaking ingenuity in their erotic pursuits. The results can be breathtaking also in a painful way, or in clumsy or poignant ways, like the invention of the situationship. Love in the time of algorithms, as Dan Slater narrates the rise of dating apps, substitutes for permanence in a relationship the permanence of the quest. Dating apps offer their own kind of never-ending promise, not union with a person you love until you die, but the expectation that you can always find someone better out there. That plus streaming porn was sufficient to dissolve manners around dating, courting, and marrying, and to reframe sex as predominantly transactional.[22]

It does not seem entirely strange that people would choose marriage as an exit from that landscape even if they enjoyed it while living there. Nevertheless the perks of single life are considerable enough that, to leave it behind, men and women may really have to be convinced that they are getting something better. An optimized marriage might seem the only kind worth entering. This kind of marriage sometimes gets billed as an advanced species of friendship. It is a little different from the 1990s ideal of best friends who are lovers. Thirty years later the ideal spouse is someone beloved because he or she boosts what one loves best about oneself. Marrying your "soulmate" or "your person" or the one who makes you "feel seen" reverses antique paradigms of marriage as one-flesh union or reunion with one's better half. Instead, as highbrow people might best exemplify, one person leagues to another who will enjoy how fabulous she is and make her better. Eli Finkel identifies this as an "all-or-nothing" marriage.[23]

That dazzling kind of marriage may sound great if you can get it and if you can keep it. But many people can't get it and others can't keep it. The instability might be a feature, not a bug. Critics of this marital type have built up whole cottage industries devoted to dumping cold water on newlywed soulmates. In 2020, sociologist W. Bradford Wilcox declared the death of "soulmate marriage," with good riddance. Dismissing "me-first marriage," Wilcox champions stable unions statistically proven to yield better outcomes as measured by health, wealth, and the next generation, a "family-first marriage." He predicts the soulmate model will "largely die off" in the face of adversities. Twenty-first-century marriage boosters do tend to sort into the two camps Wilcox describes. The soulmate love story sounds great but it's a fairy tale, say family-first proponents. Then again, pitching the family-first model to me-first singles is more vinegar than honey. The girl must live, so why marry?[24]

Of course, combining the romantic and the domestic is not always straightforward. Some writers in the past have worried that husbands and wives should keep some distance, that too much proximity or similarity breeds disgust for lovers. For people who worry about disgust, embodiment is usually the problem. More than one writer blames bacon. Jean-Jacques

---

22. Parker-Pope, "Masks, No Kissing;" Slater, *Love in the Time of Algorithms*.
23. Finkel, *The All-or-Nothing Marriage*; Mintz, *Prime of Life*, 141.
24. Wilcox, *Get Married*, and "Soulmate Marriage, RIP."

Friends and Lovers (Marriage)

Rousseau (1712–1778) thought men and women should cultivate remoteness from each other to keep love from sinking beneath the quotidian slog of "feeding slop to the pigs, draining the bacon grease, or squirting ketchup on a shirt," in Scott Yenor's pungent summary of Rousseau's theory. About two centuries later, with breakfast pork still anaphrodisiac, Marabel Morgan defends a husband's dismay that his "once sexy bride is now wrapped in rollers and smells like bacon and eggs." Surely now that men and women are so good at being friends, eros-energized marriages should be strong enough thrive in the daily grind.[25]

Religious tradition has some resources to make this vision more appealing. Though sermons at church weddings too often conceal the fact, Christianity has wisdom on marriage beyond disapproval of breaking it or having sex outside it. Christians have contributed much to shaping popular imagination of weddings, from liturgies offering phrases like "for better for worse, in sickness and in health" to vernacular speech, to chapels and bells providing a default nuptial aesthetic. Inspiration from Christian sources now less often frames popular sensibilities about the period before a wedding, what used to be called courtship. This is too bad. Cultural Christian behavior around dating is easy to mock: purity ceremonies and elaborate rules for keeping libido in check, but an admirable lot of fun can rise from the wit of young people fond of each other and intent on those diversions.

Christians conserve the very attributes that have drawn people conventionally outside eligibility for marriage to want it. St. Augustine named the goods of marriage as *proles* (having children), *fides* (faithfulness), and *sacramentum* (indissoluble union). Christianity has its own fine idioms for marriage as a special friendship, spouses as fellow pilgrims, as companions and helpers. For their part, Protestants have lots to say in favor of marriage beyond its healing scourge of mutual sanctification or its vulnerability to breakfast odors. Marriage is metaphor for Christ's union with believers. Churches also help build bridges between the private enclosure of a couple's love and the world around. Congregations at weddings make their own vow to support the newlyweds in their union.[26]

Union with all its component parts is the reason why marriage is still worth doing when one does not have to do it. Unions are somewhat out of fashion. Rather than choosing a bond with one person forever for the sharing of home, land, work, money, bed, bodies, and babies, optimized

---

25. Yenor, *Family Politics*, 5, 58; Morgan, *Total Woman*, 92.
26. Witte, *From Sacrament to Contract*, 21–23.

marriage aims to be primarily about love. The "me-first" love-match centers on the egalitarian enjoyment of two people who are defined by the jobs and hobbies that merited the other's swipe right. In fact, most people do not seek marriage only for love's sake, but now try to put together a package of their own design. Frustratingly though, when pieces of the marriage package are acquired separately, assembling them can be tricky. Pieces tend to come in mismatched sizes and not fit together well. Parties in a me-first marriage often keep strong individual identities, sharing leisure in common while farming out the other household duties to the market. That is exactly the wrong way to optimize felicity. The untapped wellspring for marital well-being may be that very part often cast aside, chores. Housework, like love, is an embodied reality. A twenty-first-century version of the victory of love over marriage might achieve that combination of ingredients medieval people couldn't get to stick, romantic and domestic love. That combination should be easier to achieve now that many chores have gone artisanal, now that bright people boast skill at making sourdough or compost.

Choosing the assembled package, love and work together, has merits. Not only is it actually sensible to combine companionship, attraction, collaboration, childrearing, and finances, but the bundle becomes itself a bonus. The bundle may even be the point. Literature scholar Devorah Baum observes that many weddings, like her own, not only place the bride and the groom in a garden setting but invite the assembled guests too into this romantic space, into the couple's "grove," their love remaking a kind of paradise. The couple deserves its romantic friendship, but its goods should reach back to the people who helped them get together, the people posed up and down St. Mary's back stairs.[27]

In her own life, Baum had understandable distrust for an institution loaded with its "surfeit of historical abuses," but she still found herself unquestionably wanting to get married: "if not this, if not marriage and children, then what?" The pair makes something beyond the pair. This abundance, not just prudery or hard-nosed counting of fieldhands, is why children long have been cherished among the goods of married life. Children are good in themselves and they also present living symbols of two lives so closely woven together that the strands could not be teased apart, beyond the sum of what each party brought in.[28]

---

27. Baum, *On Marriage*, 22, 46.
28. Baum, *On Marriage*, 4.

Chapter 5

Naked I Came (Birth)

NAKED I CAME INTO the world and naked will I leave it. That's the condition for all humans, for the Bible tells me so. The second half of that is true. Experience casts doubt on the first part. We may be born without clothes on, but the baby leaves the womb wearing the vernix, a milky coat on the skin that robes the creature from the cold outside. A baby making passage down the birth canal gets wrapped in a microbiome, the first fitting of a garment each of us wears lifelong. Newborn babies only look naked. In American hospitals until recently, nurses used to scrub the vernix from newborn babies before handing the baby to the parents. Now the practice is to leave it on. After all, it seems a little strange to scrub off the residue of Mother in order to make baby presentable to Mother.

A woman has swaddled the new-souled creature in three layers by the time it comes from her: the flesh of its body, the vernix, and the microbiome. At some point we are nothing and then at some point we are something. We do not make up that something. Some grow up moving whenever their people pull up tent stakes, moving along with their moving world. Many of us get born into something and make a way from where we start. We arrive in the world in a particular place at a particular time, all of that documented carefully on a form telling who we are. The garments of time and place stand ready for each baby pushed into the world, how the air feels then and the events going on in the world and the intentions of adults who mark those events as important. The new person slips arms and legs into that garment as she slips from her mother. When other people see us, they see us clothed in this garment. How old are you? Where are you from? What are your people like? What did natality write on your mortal frame?

The clingy cloaks a baby comes out wearing are fact before they turn metaphor. Most birth metaphors disappoint. Birth should interest everyone less as a metaphor and more as physical fact, as in, wow, can you believe this is how we come to be? The adult penchant to pluck metaphors for later bits of life from that all-important moment that none of us remembers shows how inadequate is our cultural processing of birth. After the story of salvation, the most interesting thing there is in the world is how one person walks around holding another whole person in her innards, a complete stranger, while her own body bursts without breaking. Birth is fundamental to embodied life.

A SHORT HISTORY OF AMERICAN BIRTH

Early American parents and birth attendants inherited some of their ideas about reproduction from ancient Greeks. In the American colonies, an early popular reproductive-health manual (sex book plus midwifery guide) was *Aristotle's Masterpiece*, not written by Aristotle but still indebted to him and his anatomical misunderstandings, reinterpreted through centuries of puzzling over some biological facts Americans now take for granted. Ancient Greeks and Romans trying to understand where babies come from said they came from seeds. Some of these ancient theorists thought both men and women had seeds, and some thought only men did. In any case, most theorists agreed that men were responsible for the real work of making a new person come to be. The woman might provide the raw matter, warm wet holding place, but otherwise was inert as dirt. Long-held theories of maternal impressions suggested mothers could interfere with gestation by "impressing" their bad thoughts on the baby, or by staring at scary animals or eating wrong foods, marking the baby or miscarrying it. But otherwise the woman's task mostly was not to mess up what man made or God wrought. This general idea persisted into Europe well past the microscope's invention and eventual discovery of gametes, fertilization, and fetal development.[1]

When birth came due, women summoned a midwife, a woman trained by expertise and practice to help at delivery and attend the birthing mother. The new mother usually had other women during a period of confinement to prepare food and manage household tasks and infant care. Delivery by midwife had high rates of safe birth. Social childbirth provided

1. Fissell, "Hairy Women and Naked Truths."

support, though it would be a mistake for past or present to assume all deliveries were easy or happy. Men thought a lot about reproduction and offspring—they wrote most of the books about those topics—but stayed at some distance from birth itself until, in late seventeenth and early eighteenth centuries, the man-midwife brought tools and status to compete with traditional birth personnel.[2]

In the United States, most births happened at home until well into the twentieth century, attended by midwife or family physician. In the early twentieth century, a new national agency, the US Children's Bureau, sought to reduce infant mortality by investigating its sources and providing education, in the form of prenatal care guidebooks for mothers. A novel approach, prenatal care emerged from doctors' observation that a few birth emergencies could be anticipated and avoided by monitoring the expectant mother, testing for syphilis or checking blood pressure and urine. A woman's overall health, good diet, and exercise could make birth smoother. By mid-twentieth century, study of nutrients and endocrine systems kept adding more knowledge to prenatal care and more tasks too, not only things for doctor to watch but things for the expectant mother to do. The bargain was that if she entrusted her pregnancy to her doctor, following his rules and doing what he advised, she would have a better birth and a healthier baby.[3]

Birth can hurt, and plenty of women were glad to have it hurt less. Doctors piloted obstetric anesthesia in the nineteenth century by holding a handkerchief doused in chloroform over the mother's face. In the early twentieth century twilight sleep was briefly popular, a pain-management method in which the laboring mother felt pain but forgot it. The combination of drugs for twilight sleep could leave mothers flailing during labor so they were restrained with blindfolds and straitjackets. After one of its American enthusiasts died during a twilight-sleep birth in 1915, the method fell out of fashion. By the 1950s, hospitals instead eliminated birth pain with general anesthesia.[4]

American women increasingly left home to have babies in the twentieth century. Push and pull factors both contributed to moving birth to hospitals. State laws and doctors' guilds marginalized midwives, sometimes nastily. Some women found medical care and its institutions more convenient, more fashionable. Nevertheless doctors could not actually guarantee

2. Ulrich, *Midwife's Tale*; Wertz and Wertz, *Lying-In*.
3. Walzer, *Brought to Bed*; Howard, "Changing Expectation."
4. Wolf, *Deliver Me from Pain*.

a healthy baby. Medical supervision of birth was itself fraught with dangers. For example, some drugs doctors prescribed for pregnancy complications harmed women and babies. DES (diethylstilbestrol), a synthetic estrogen, caused cancer and fertility problems for women and babies exposed to it. Thalidomide, given to European women for morning sickness and anxiety, caused fetal deformities like missing limbs or failing organs. Though, thankfully, thalidomide was never licensed in the United States, press coverage of these disasters troubled the reliance American women increasingly invested in obstetrics. Even scrupulous prenatal self-management could not guarantee a good time in labor. By mid-century most American babies were born in hospitals. In hospitals, mothers-to-be could birth in antiseptic conditions and avail antibiotics in case of infection. Perhaps even more important to shaping the experience, a woman could birth without pain through use of anesthesia. In common mid-century procedure, a woman arrived at a hospital in labor, was rendered unconscious, and then awakened all stitched up and with a new baby ready for beholding.[5]

Some mid-twentieth-century birth reformers objected to this medicalization. Grantly Dick-Read, Fernand Lamaze, and Robert Bradley recommended gentler and more prepared versions of natural birth for which women would not need anesthesia. Natural childbirth also rallied feminists in the 1970s, Boston movement leaders cobbling together *Our Bodies, Ourselves* to help women reclaim their own health care. Midwifery pioneer Ina May Gaskin settled The Farm in Tennessee to train midwives and welcome sometimes psychedelic births. The next decades shifted culture so far from assembly-line hospital births to more natural, less medicalized ones that by the 1990s, one might have guessed that the norm for births would find women lounging in bathtubs in their own homes, a midwife and a doula and supportive female friends around to help the baby come in its own sweet time.[6]

Instead, having been warned what to expect when they were expecting, American women entered upon more thorough medical supervision. The logic of prenatal care, the advancements in reproductive technology, and the acceptance of epidural anesthesia redirected moms emphatically back to medical specialists and hospitals. By the late twentieth century, women were presumed to be learning a lot from books. American pregnancy became "constructed as a reading assignment," Cristina Mazzoni writes, such that "pregnant women need[ed] instructions in order to participate in

---

5. Epstein, *Get Me Out*, 109–28.
6. Rothman, *Bun in the Oven*, 104–11; Kline, *Coming Home*, 64–94.

their own pregnancy." The iconic book series, *What to Expect When You're Expecting*, offered women month-by-month notes about fetal development and wellness, translating obstetricians' advice to language accessible to the laywoman. The book was supposed to reassure women but many read its tips as fearmongering. The prospect that some maternal acts could enhance fetal health implied the reverse, that other actions could inflict harm. Suddenly a pregnant woman had many rules to obey, the flouting of which could impose suffering on a child's entire future life. *What to Expect* books and their myriad imitators are not specifically to blame for these risk calculations. Those books follow out the logic of prenatal care.[7]

Rather than putting prenatal management into a woman's own hands, these books impelled deference to doctors' orders While women's empowerment seemed to be the goal of prenatal care manuals, the effect of more information about pregnancy often was not to spark wonder or enjoyment. Instead, information sensitized mothers to what could go wrong. In popular minds, OBs appeared to be the people who could avert disaster. Prenatal care tied a double bind. By the 1990s, women seemed to be participating more fully in their pregnancies, doing the tasks doctors assigned, invited to write their own birth plans, but doctors rather than mothers received credit for successful delivery. Women had to do much to ensure a baby's health but could be made to feel they were never doing enough.[8]

Women pregnant in the last decade of the twentieth century and first decades of the next faced cross-cutting pressures. The task of carrying a fetus appeared risky and complicated and therefore in need of medical supervision. Even before pregnancy, a woman might need a doctor to assist fertility or to monitor progress, then to manage the pregnancy and deliver a baby with machines only available in hospitals By 2020, close to a third of births in the United States were nudged along with induction and a third were born by cesarean section. Natural-birth and midwifery advocates offered critique of aggressive intervention that resonated with some women. But American mothers often were told hospitals provide safety and best care for their babies. Hospitals sensitive to market trends redesigned maternity facilities with cozy furniture, a compromise that brought a generation of American babies into the world in homelike delivery suites, with monitors and needles at the ready right behind a curtain. Pendulum swings from

---

7. Mazzoni, *Maternal Impressions*, 65; Eisenberg, Murkoff, and Hathaway, *What to Expect*.

8. Howard, *Showing*, 73–80.

excessive intervention to insistence on natural birth nudged some moms to feel like they fell short no matter what they did.[9]

When American pregnancy was turning into a reading assignment in the late twentieth century, it also was turning into a science experiment. Research revealed features of reproduction that humans never knew before. Discoveries about ovulation and hormones produced new contraceptives. While birth control—sex without babies—was the great leap of reproductive medicine in the 1960s, the 1970s and 1980s produced technology to make babies without sex. Louise Brown, the world's first "test-tube baby" conceived through successful in-vitro fertilization (IVF), was born in England in 1978. Elizabeth Carr, the first American IVF baby, came in 1981. Australian parents in 1984 welcomed the first baby born from a frozen egg. Sperm donation, egg donation, and surrogacy employed the pioneering technologies to make babies in ways unimaginable before, for those who could not have been prospective birthing parents before, same-sex couples and postmenopausal women.[10]

Around the turn of the twenty-first century, high-profile treatments for infertility, assisted reproductive technologies (ARTs), births of multiples, and surrogacy caught public attention and broader usage. Ethical questions surrounded ARTs, contending over the right way to get and use gametes and embryos, the commercial character of their "donation," and the nature of parenthood when babies could be made through something besides sex. The 1986 Baby M case displayed pitfalls of surrogacy when the woman hired to gestate a child resisted parting with the baby, courts ultimately awarding custody to the contracting parents. The President's Council on Bioethics, convened in 2001 by George W. Bush, seemed for a while to exist chiefly to argue about embryos, how to make them, how to freeze them, who owned them, when they should be treated as human. Though the prospect of genetic modification, especially with the CRISPR technique, opened yearning and worry over "designer" babies, the fear near the top of most lists remained cloning. In decades closing the century, controversies roiled.[11]

Remarkably, in the decades opening the twenty-first century, controversies mostly settled down as technological accomplishments kept on

---

9. Simpson, "Trends in Labor Induction"; Stephenson, "Rate of First-time Cesarean"; Jones, *Matrescence*.

10. Mundy, *Everything Conceivable*; Spar, *Baby Business*.

11. President's Council on Bioethics, "Human Cloning and Human Dignity;" Smajdor and Deech, *From IVF to Immortality*.

coming. Some people earlier worried that reproductive technology would not only change the way people made babies but the way they thought about making them. It did. ARTs became normal. Thousands of IVF babies have been born in the US.[12]

Technology offered solutions to uncertainties about reproduction. Technology proved able to enhance male and female body parts involved in making a baby, to start a baby one place and put it somewhere else to gestate, to screen embryo or fetus for genetic abnormalities and even edit away abnormalities, to show parents a fetus hidden in the womb. Parents now can have a baby of their own despite infertility. A single person can choose to have a child without a partner. Baby-making only has anything to do with sex when people choose to make it that way.

BIRTH IN LIVED EXPERIENCE

At the start of the twentieth century, Progressive reformers in the United States campaigned for birth registration on grounds that states must know how many babies were born in order to help their citizens, or to regulate, tax, or draft them. I know details of my grandmother's birth only because I found her birth certificate. My grandmother was born in Cleveland in 1906, a Slovak midwife attending her mother at their small apartment. Her mother was twenty-five years old when she was born. The handwritten registration card reports the "nativity" of both father and mother as "Ungar, Austria." Two years later my grandfather was born, just across the border from Ohio in Pennsylvania. A Slavic midwife attended his mother too, then aged twenty. Both of his parents are described simply as being Hungarian. The father's occupation is listed as miner, the mother's as housewife. None of my grandparents actually is Hungarian, another reminder that our parents and our time clothe us before any other garment at birth.[13]

My mother's birth was my grandmother's third. Those first three were done at her parents' farmhouse. My grandmother's first-born son lived only a few days, just long enough for his baptism. My grandfather had been at work when the baby died. When he came home he heard the news and cried, and the doctor slapped his face and told him to get hold of himself.

---

12. HHS Fact Sheet, "In Vitro Fertilization (IVF) Use Across the US."

13. The birth registrar symbolically returned them to the Austro-Hungarian empire then ruling over their territory, the land that would become Czechoslovakia in 1918 and Slovakia in 1993.

During the wake, when men were playing cards in the kitchen to keep vigil with the casket, a light glowed around it suddenly and onlookers received this as the child's thanks for his baptism. Another son followed and then my mother was delivered by the same doctor in that farmhouse bedroom.

My mother had her first pregnancy in the year after she was married. Her doctor worried about difficult delivery and so performed a cesarean section. In that era one cesarean usually required subsequent births to be done that way too. The doctor advised my mother that she could have more children if she went ahead soon, and she did with four more. My mother never described her pregnancies beyond the doctor's management and her good health. About birth there was not much story either, since we all were surgically removed while she was under anesthesia. Thus, like much else in childhood, all our stories were mostly a single story. What my mother could tell us about was the procedure and the scars. The doctors put a long needle in her back. They cut her abdomen open and stitched her up. That was birth. Cesarean incisions then were not the "bikini cut" but a line from navel on down, bisecting the belly. When she woke from anesthesia, nurses told her whether she had a boy or a girl.

We all were breastfed, feed-on-demand babies. I demanded a lot. I was born just over five pounds but dropped a few ounces so registered as underweight. The hospital put me in an incubator. The floor nurse who brought me to my mother when I awakened crying named me Mighty Mouse because I was small and loud. I gained ounces, they brought me home, and the nickname returned from time to time. It did not occur to me for at least fifty years to put together the facts that I was born small and by a scheduled c-section. That is, I was the doctor's mistake. There were no ultrasounds at that time to check. Still, he might have known. The crying and craving, the incubator days, all what it cost, came to me because he counted wrong and then took up the knife.

Birthing and babies did not interest me in childhood. In grad school I stumbled onto pregnancy as historical phenomenon. I read about potions of roots and herbs fed to expectant women and about eyeballing their urine to discern whether the coming child was boy or girl. One of the best books about early New England women tells of a Maine midwife and her world. In real life at the same time, I was hearing talk about babies and births in the context of male grad-student colleagues who would say, "we're pregnant" to announce when wives were expecting babies. The pregnant women told me how weird it was not to be able to drink coffee or to feel like their bodies were being taken over by an alien. This timing of discoveries about pregnancy was favorable since I recently married and my husband and I were thinking about having a family. I pledged never to say "we" were pregnant.

When I got pregnant everything seemed like a big deal. I bought a pregnancy test at the drug store, a big deal. I discovered it was positive, a big deal. I surprised my husband with the news on his birthday, a big deal. I had blood drawn, a big deal because I am a fainter. My body changed, a big deal. I felt nauseated, my least favorite kind of sickness. My gut grew and my skin got blotchy and a dark line appeared running down from my belly button, which looked to me like a prefiguration of the cesarean scar that gave me life, a big deal.

When I went to the OB for a first visit, nothing was a big deal. In most ways that was a good thing. Business as usual means nothing is wrong. Business as usual means that bringing babies safely into the world is in fact the obstetrician's business. But I was perplexed. *What to Expect* ran a notoriously tight ship warning women to be careful about everything—food, cleaning products, cosmetics, cat litter, advising them on all that could go wrong if moms-to-be did not discipline their behavior. Everything seemed like a big deal in the world of *What to Expect,* big and mostly bad. A mom-to-be had to know and do stuff. After reading the book in the privacy of my own home, I found it disconcerting for nurses in the OB office to smile and say everything was fine, to give me no stern to-do list or no dire warnings.

Again, that take-it-easy approach can be a good thing. By twenty-first-century pregnancies, moms learned to cast a cool eye on to-do lists. Some mothers reject the obstetrical double-bind of worry and vigilance. Baby safety is a doctor's job, after all. Even so, I left prenatal appointments deflated. I knew being pregnant was a big deal. I woke up every morning not my regular self but a walking community. A stranger had moved into my house and slept in my bed, making me both the bed and the house, and the kitchen and dumpster too. My doctor and my nurses did not necessarily have to be the ones to stand agape at that fact, but they were the people whom pregnancy sent me to and I didn't have anyone else. It surprised me too that other people were not wide-eyed and obsessed with the events occurring in my torso, not on my account but from sheer wonder at the unfolding of life.

This body, until these months fairly unremarkable and fairly functional, was hardly recognizable to me. It morphed: here a lump, there a line, legs heavy, ankles swollen, hair more lush. Pregnancy discombobulates, even easy pregnancies. I did not have heartburn or hyperemesis, did not throw my back out. But I lived day to day with no idea how my body would feel, not because I lacked information about what was happening to it but because I had no control over it. The weird things that happened to my body seemed to have no logical connection to what was happening in my uterus. Nobody tried to explain that mismatch either. The doctor and the guidebooks indicated what organ the baby was developing around now, what size and shape the baby attained this month, but did not explain why, say, I would feel nauseated when the baby was growing a heart, or get pimply when the baby's toenails were getting longer. My medical guides made no effort whatsoever to connect my experience with the baby's development, even though all that development was happening inside my experience.

I first felt my first baby move when sitting in a theater watching a play, and the whole universe opened up. I forget the play for how strange it was to have some other person move limbs inside my body and to be aware of what it was, my sensory parts telling my brain because the books had told me, "that is the baby kicking," so I could interpret myself to myself. I was also interpreting that other person to myself, what parents do for the rest of kids' lives, though I did not know that person yet and was only pretending to know her, because books and the doctor told me the baby kicked when I drank juice or ate something spicy. I knew what the fetus was doing but not what she was thinking. Did she know what I was doing or thinking?

Somebody gave me a book on praying for your baby in utero. I did it, but this was not the most obvious way pregnancy might make a person think about God. Christians sometimes apply verses from Scripture to maternal encouragement. I was willing to believe that God was knitting a person in my abdomen. If that were what was happening, though, that would be an astonishing visitation from God right there in my gut. If God were putting together a baby whom God made, in my gut, my prayers *for* that seemed hardly necessary. When I prayed I already was praying *with* that person because that person was in me and could not escape my prayers if she tried. I marveled to be a person carrying around two eternal souls. I marveled that nobody treated me as if that were true or as amazing as it actually is, not the person on the street, not the OB nurses, not my priest.

Pregnancy in America had turned into reading assignment, as the scholar said. The assigned reading I found was not the right kind. I wanted books to tell what pregnancy meant, like a story or theology, what is God making? Instead the reading assignment mostly entailed bossy books that told women just enough for nine months of felt inadequacy. The reading assignment of the 1990s was a shelf full mostly all saying the same things, this one more clinical, that one scolding pregnant gals to be more sexy. This refrain got worse when social media took over assigning the readings. That said, a lot of excellent books have been written about pregnancy and birth in the last two decades. American women now have the kind of pregnancy reading assignment I wanted.[14]

When I went to my prenatal care appointments, I wanted the OB staff to say, a marvel! You are carrying around a new person, a person never before seen in the universe! You two are making a single-use organ together, glory to the placenta! Those would have been right exclamations for this thing that was happening in my body. But I thought a share of praise should come to me too because I was doing so dutifully what I was supposed to do. I was accomplishing something. I was accomplishing a person, a stranger who puttered around the house with me and sat up straight when I went to type at the computer. Sometimes she kicked me. I woke up in mornings not just to go write words but to make whole new organs for a person I didn't know. I could have made whole new organs I did not even have myself, in the event the girl turned out to be a boy.

A few OB visits had thrills built in, like hearing a heartbeat that was not my own come pounding out of my body. The first ultrasound was thrilling, I guess, although my husband and I had decided not to be told the baby's sex in an era when telling that news was standard. I tried so hard not to see the sex that I am not sure I saw very much of anything. Ultrasounds were generally disappointing, at least in days of clumsy technology and blurry resolution, the baby a blobby brown and the only really discernible part the spine That is a beautiful part, though, pearls on a string.

It was dumb for me to expect amazement from doctors and nurses. But it ought to come from somebody, and the way pregnancy was set up in late twentieth-century America, doctors' offices were where a person went to have a pregnancy managed. Why not praised and honored too? A fast runner finds a coach, a piano prodigy finds a music teacher; those who want to lose weight or stop drinking find groups and advisers to coax the new work of the body and applaud its good changes. Pregnant women get doctors as the ones who are supposed to help them because doctors know about pregnancy. Nurses and midwives and doulas do this work too. Who else is there? Public marvel ought to come from somewhere. The OB office

---

14. Ours is a golden age for readers interested in pregnancy and birth. Among the many excellent books addressing aspects for academic and general readers, see Banks, *Natality*; Hazard, *Womb*; Carnes, *Motherhood*; Adams and Lundquist, eds., *Coming to Life*.

is the one that handled and judged my pregnancies. In the coin of their realm, the better kind of attention was no attention, no news was good news.

For the first birth I lived so close to the hospital that I intended to walk there for labor. That was my birth plan. Like many women's birth plans, that did not work out. The efficient part of labor started around midnight and walking was less appealing then. Late the next morning my daughter was born. I have made a man with God's help, I wanted to shout to the nurses. A mere few days later I was startled that the hospital would let me leave in my condition, oozing blood and obviously not a competent mother, but nurses wheeled me to the car and then the rest was up to us. We buckled the baby into the car seat wrong.

My first time was not a standout birth story. My other two births were not great stories either. I consented to inductions. I didn't feel like I could refuse. I had a plan that I would play "Ave Maria" through a speaker and join my labor to the incarnation. I did not do that. Births, specifically my hospital births, were not all that great. Having those babies born and alive and well was great. But pregnancy was in all respects the more interesting part of childbearing.

I loved being pregnant. I did not suffer the severe symptoms some women do. Like many, I finished the experience stretched, saggy, scarred. No one should make light of the distress some women face through pregnancy and birth. Still, distress does not cancel out astonishment. Distress might make any particular woman dislike her pregnancy but it should get the attention of the rest of us in ways that easy breezy pregnancies sometimes obscure.

I loved being pregnant, but at least two of my pregnancies ended in miscarriage. One required a hospital procedure in a labor-and-delivery ward, where I delivered a baby we knew was no longer living, surrounded by OB personnel and other mothers doing live births. It felt like a cruel setting. If ever reminder were necessary that the way Americans handle "normal" births prepares or fails to prepare for hard cases, this time showed me. All three of my living babies spent their first night in plastic bassinets in the nursery down the hall on a labor-delivery hospital wing so I could rest. The size of my body's accomplishment, making a person with no small spending of blood and toil, earned me rest.

Naked I Came (Birth)
WHAT'S STRANGE ABOUT AMERICAN BIRTH

What's strange about birth in the United States is the gigantic apparatus that functions to remind passersby of its dangers. Imagining birth as difficult or dangerous should bother twenty-first-century Americans. In some respects, birth has become easier, maybe easier than ever in the history of the world. Before scientific discoveries and medical breakthroughs, babies existed because their parents had sex. Parents knew little about the kinds of babies they would have. They had little ability to space or pace their children or enhance the health of offspring. For those who wanted babies but could not have them, options favored adoption or foster care. Women who got pregnant from sex without social approval were exposed and shamed by the fact of their single motherhood. When birth attendants were untrained and lacked necessary medicines, mothers and babies could die from preventable causes. Ignorance, fatalism, shame, and dread stand guilty of stifling the astonishment due to the fact of pregnancy and birth.

Knowledge and technology now make it possible to avoid, plan, or achieve conception despite infertility; to monitor and enhance gestation; to keep women healthy and employed during pregnancy; to deliver babies reliably, even on chosen schedules, in safe spaces with less pain or nearly none; to prevent postpartum infection and many perinatal dangers. Scientific progress brought some real benefits to birth by the mid-twentieth century, antiseptics reducing external contaminations, antibiotics ending infections, anesthesia making it possible to blunt pain, safety built by personnel and institutions overseeing birth. All that might have added up to progress, birth made so safe and comfortable that mothers and others could witness its magnitude, awe no longer drained by pain or fear. Under these conditions, motherhood might be flourishing in quality and quantity, at least among mothers who have access to those benefits.

Instead, the prospect of having a child may feel more fraught now than in my baby-bearing years or my mother's or grandmother's. Technology changed how babies are made. Society and economy have changed conditions around women's imagining and doing motherhood. Women who would like to have children may struggle to assemble the preconditions. Choice sets the table with ambivalence, the decision to have children or not complicated and politically loaded, an option that can interfere with the bunch of other happy things one has made with one's life. Professional trajectories make timing of motherhood tricky. Even women content with traditional-seeming sequences of college, marriage, work, and motherhood may find partners for that project elusive. With gender disparities in higher education and mating practices rigged against long relationships, a good man can be hard to find, especially one who envisions fatherhood as attractive. To preserve their prospects, women may choose to have eggs extracted and frozen for the future. Men disposed to fatherhood may be discouraged from broaching the topic out of deference on reproductive questions, or perhaps from the absence of children in their everyday lives.[15]

For couples who confront infertility, ARTs may create babies but can also raise then frustrate hopes and reconfigure parenthood. Popular donors at sperm banks can generate dozens or hundreds of children with unclear relational or legal ties, implying that genetics determine children and also that traits can be abstracted from parents' contribution. Commercialization is more egregious still in the economics of surrogacy, especially international surrogacy, where intended parents from wealthy countries contract to gestate fetuses in vulnerable women across the globe.[16]

Even when both partners want children and can conceive, complications multiply. Some couples choose to have no children or fewer than desired because they fear they cannot afford them or because they hope to spare offspring planetary disaster. Some couples want children but not very badly, maybe less than other adult pursuits. Since having children is a choice, social expectation can leave parents solely responsible for their rearing. Analysts with an eye to demography worry that shrinking birth rates will wreak havoc on institutions before long, but tax breaks and childcare subsidies have not been sufficient to change minds. Challenges to birth look much more intimidating than scientific progress might have indicated.[17]

The medical-scientific narrative has not worked its magic on imagination of pregnancy either. Modern science revealed jaw-dropping things about human reproduction. Too often those facts fuel anxiety rather than amazement. Birth remains mostly in the ambit of doctors in health-care systems rife with problems. In this decade, more hospitals have closed labor-delivery departments as too costly to maintain. Too much or the wrong kind of intervention can leave mothers-to-be disempowered or traumatized. Too little can be tragic. US rates of maternal mortality are surprisingly high, in part from lapses in attention to the health of mothers. Hospital deliveries can be lifesaving for some women and babies but are

15. Berg and Wiseman, *What Are Children For?*; Inhorn, *Motherhood on Ice*, 1–21.
16. Lewis, "Surrogacy as Feminism" and *Full Surrogacy Now*; Bowles, "Sperm Kings."
17. Van der Lugt, *Begetting*; Carney, *Family Unfriendly*.

costly and distort expectations when structured as the default. Science and medicine remedy dangers but create new complications with birth as well burying worthy questions about birth by the spectacle of seeming mastery.[18]

Women resisting high-tech, assembly-line deliveries in the late twentieth century reshaped culture around birth. That cultural shift left twenty-first-century moms sometimes feeling bullied by the high standards of naturalness, feeling judged as inferior if they chose epidurals or surgeries or opted out of exclusive breastfeeding. Having the natural as preferential option could be read as a victory for birth reform. But some close students of birth culture interpret this pressure on women as manipulation and disrespect, no less than their mothers a generation before interpreted high-tech interventions this way.[19]

Technology offers itself to relieve the bodily trouble of childbearing. Soon, maybe in a generation or so, bodily mess can be eliminated altogether by fertilizing eggs in a petri dish, then growing embryos in glass, then outsourcing pregnancy to artificial wombs from which babies can be removed and handed over clean to the parents who contracted for them. It would not surprise at all to discover this disembodied manner of producing new humans presented as a great breakthrough, even as liberation [20]

Disembodied birth would not be liberation for women. Though it is desirable to make aspects of childbearing less painful or perilous to mothers, it is not desirable to throw out the baby-making with the bathwater. The imperfection of birth experience does not invite the elimination of birth experience. Giving embodied hospitality to new-forming people is a worthy practice, for parents and children and humanity. Because public conversations are not fluent in evaluating pregnancy and birth well, they stammer to express the problems of something like ectogenesis, birth from artificial wombs. Americans should get more articulate about what is not just mammalian but good about the old way of making babies.

When children were inevitable and pregnancy was mysterious and maybe dangerous, the need was to make the process safer and support women through it. When children were still pretty much expected and the process made safer, the need was to make pregnancy more comfortable and more compatible with women's other pursuits. By the late twentieth century, American women were initiated to assuming pregnancy a healthy process, with problems the exception. Then, American culture might have

18. Kliff, "Most Rural Hospitals Have Closed"; Hoyert, "Maternal Mortality Rates."
19. Jones, *Matrescence*, 61–62, 64.
20. Horn, "Ectogenesis Is for Feminists."

found ways to marvel at the phenomenon of a person having another person in the belly. American rhetoric mostly privatizes pregnancy, makes it girlfriendy or clinical or clownish. As pregnancy becomes a rarer experience, fewer women having fewer babies, its place in human experience could shift dramatically. On one hand, when adults are ambivalent about having children at all, eliminating barriers to entry might make it attractive to eliminate pregnancy altogether. Ambivalent parenthood abstracted from relationships or sex could logically lean to ectogenesis. On the other hand, if artificial wombs become popular, old-fashioned birth could become a sought-after event, like a luxury good or an extreme sport, that dazzling show of bringing a baby out of one's body.

What's strange about the way Americans birth is confusion of the terms and help of the wrong variety. What's strange is that technology, celebrity attention, and feminine empowerment failed to normalize honor around birth. What's strange is that Americans lapse easily into the language of reproductive health, loquacious about sex, contraception, or abortion, but speak so haltingly about reproduction itself.

BETTER THINKING ABOUT BIRTH

The birth environment around my new motherhood seemed to solve many problems people perennially confront. The future appeared to make birth safe and happy and give women choice and control. Instead emphasis fell wrong in each category. Safety measures raised risk awareness and anxiety. Full control was never really part of baby-making. Dependence on doctors undermined women's trust in their own judgment and body in labor, but rhetoric of the natural bullied mothers too. Leaning the other way might have stressed the significance of birth and honored women's work in it rather than using the natural as the placeholder for the good of female embodiment, and safety as shorthand for all the assistance women ought to get in bringing forth new life.

Birth is a big deal. The fact that human beings enter the world from the body of another person is unremarkable only to those who never have considered it. As Jennifer Banks writes, we are "fundamentally natal creatures," and therefore it is appropriate that "throughout our lives we will be forced, whether we like it or not, to wrestle with our own natality."[21]

---

21. Banks, *Natality*, 5.

Naked I Came (Birth)

Humans not only enter the world from another person but, as far as the unaided eye can see, they go from non-being to full-bodied existence within the body of another person who does not know whom or how they will turn out to be, and a person who proceeds with her life around the fact of their taking shape. As humans, we know all mammals do this. As humans, we are unique—again, so far as we know—in being aware that we are doing this. Unlike a dog or a whale or an elephant, a human mother-to-be recognizes that the heaviness in her abdomen predicts the arrival of a new person. All the symptomatic weirdness in one's body is not just weakness or illness but immediate side effects of somebody else's existence. It is amazing that we put up with each other this way. Since we put up with each other this way, someone having extended generosity in advance, humans ought to honor this achievement when any particular woman does it. We might also be a little proud of our species that this generosity has become customary.

Generosity is evident because mothers inevitably do self-spending in pregnancy and birth. Pain comes even when things go well. When things do not go well, the fact of carrying potential for new life carries with it potential for loss. Miscarriage is common in pregnancy, affecting at least a fifth of them though likely more since much loss goes undetected. Infant and maternal mortality remain higher in the US than they should be. Obstetric anesthesiologist Donald Caton observes that some mothers-to-be in his practice opted out of anesthesia because they thought pain demonstrates that something is important. There are lots of other ways besides pain to recognize the gravity of labor. Safe delivery is hardly the end of maternal pain. That fact should not make humans refuse birth but celebrate the love in it.[22]

Parents give their kids bits of themselves. The bitter part is that parents don't get to choose the bits. Not only do we not get to select which piece of ourselves a child is spared—her nose and his hair, grandpa's predispositions and grandma's weakness—but what comes to our children sometimes we don't recognize in ourselves We may see for the first time a trait of our own in the face of the child who is both-of-us, bits shaken out of us from some pocket or closet and spilt into the makings of a child, parts we didn't know we had and do not want and would not have given as inheritance.

In my mother's birthing years, moms who were asked about hopes for the new baby were supposed to say that it wouldn't matter whether it was a

---

22. Caton, *What a Blessing She Had Chlorojorm*, ix.

boy or a girl "as long as it's healthy"—maybe nicer than the traditional answer in the era of my grandmother's births, that parents would prefer a boy. That "as long as healthy" phrase fails births that bring forth newborns who are not healthy. That line also fails as script often offered about women's laboring, that a birth is good as long as mom and baby come through it sound and alive. Maybe the shortcomings and gigantic expense of default hospital birth can be overlooked as long as mom and baby are healthy. But by the second decade of the twenty-first century too many moms and babies were not healthy. The US has higher infant mortality rates than countries of similar socioeconomic position and maternal mortality rates are worse. Reporting in 2017 showed a rise in women suffering emergencies or fatalities after birth, and the numbers are most discouraging for Black women.[23]

Some women feeling pressure to express their principles during pregnancy signal them through their healthcare choices. Regrettably, choice can be used as sufficient substitute for other ways of appreciating what birth means, a problem since choice also can be illusory. Sociologist Barbara Katz Rothman rues that medicalized childbirth prioritizes choice as consumer preference, configuring the choice of midwifery as buying an experience rather seeking midwives' skill and care.[24]

Setting the infant's safety against a mother's happy experience distorts the meaning of birth. If advised—as many mothers are advised implicitly if not in so many words—that hospital delivery is better for baby and that interest in a birth experience might verge on selfishness, most women head to the hospital. The choice cashes out not least because fashions make unclear what a good birth experience looks like. So much is at stake during birth that it can seem indulgent to care about the mom's experience. But not caring about the mom's experience endangers the whole process. Midwifery's correction to overmedicalization reminded women that birth could be powerful and meaningful, which encouraged women to invest expectation in a great birth experience. That expectation sometimes is disappointed, not just when labor complications arise but when pain or procedures make the process less thrilling than it was cracked up to be.[25]

Some postpartum letdown might come from loading too much of the wonder of making and meeting a new person onto the birth itself. Labor is a relatively short process, though it may not feel short. Labor has

23. Fields, "What to Know about Maternal Mortality;" Declercq and Zephyrin, "Maternal Mortality."

24. Rothman, *Bun in the Oven*, 127–38.

25. Jones, *Matrescence*, 68.

unpredictable timing because the body is not a machine. The nine months of pregnancy are more accommodating. During those whole months a woman probably has more time of her own to ponder, wonder, react to the prospect of the new person she alone already has met. When birth culture encourages a woman to pin all happy expectation on the part when the baby comes out, birth may be a letdown. A mom has less control over that part, in any event.

Waiting until the baby comes out to be amazed wastes those amazing nine months. In the past, maybe people talked in public less about pregnancy because they knew less of what we now know about it, and because the topic was indecent, too redolent of genitals. Women could talk to each other about pregnancy but public talk violated modesty. Now, when almost all topics enter public talk and most relate to sex, pregnancy and birth still too often function as conversational segue to something else, like ARTs or reproductive rights. What deserves attention is not just the events that bookend gestation, coitus and a birth day, but the period in between when woman and baby live as mysteries to each other.

It is understandable that other people might wait until after a baby is born to be amazed. Except for the person carrying it, a baby can seem a possibility rather than fact, a generalized phenomenon rather than this new one due one day. It is good for birth to get this attention and birth still generally does not get enough. In that pattern though, pregnancy gets slotted merely as preparation for birth. But the big experience of giving life is not just when somebody cuts the cord or lays a wet infant onto a mother's chest. Mornings spent hunched over a toilet are as vital as contractions in the labor of giving life.

Of course birth should be marked as a special occasion. Of course birth deserves the anticipation and admiration it gets, the planning about where it happens and who is present and which medicines to take or refuse. But birth is the end of something rather than only a beginning, a change in relationship and not the start of one ex nihilo. According permission to women to honor their pregnancies could take some of the pressure off of birth as the freighted experience initiating motherhood. Maybe nobody needs to give permission. Unlike birth, though, public conversations about pregnancy do not go far without getting tangled into something else.

Reticence about pregnancy also may flow from well-meant efforts to avoid loading more blame onto women. In prenatal care's pressure to optimize fetal conditions, mothers are held powerful to accomplish good things by their diet and habits. Good fetal outcomes are hard to trace to maternal diet and habits alone. Much more often traced are bad outcomes to maternal misbehaviors. One might seem the flip side of the other: women should be held responsible equally for the good and the harm they inflict on the fetus in utero. Not so. When things go wrong, moms should not be first target of blame. Given wide assumptions about women's intent to nurture the babies they hope to birth, honor should go to maternal labors, not just the outcomes. Pregnant women's painstaking, consistent, self-giving efforts deserve appreciation. Blame directed at women on suspicion they have caused fetal harm is a social phenomenon, so the corrective must be social too.[26]

Correctives might be drawn from a number of older narratives about pregnancy and birth. One kind of narrative presents the baby as a couple's tie to the past and to beloved ancestors. Another kind presents the baby as a claim to earthly immortality, parents' genes propelled glittering into the future. A narrative undergirded by Roman Catholicism presents the baby as the united love of a man and woman, the embodiment the fruit of their love. Sex has a unitive function and a procreative one, and the body of the woman is what puts the two together and where God puts them together.

It is hard to overestimate the importance of restoring a common narrative around birth, which is the foundation of our embodied life. Some of us spend lives doing metaphorically what nurses used to do physically, scrubbing off the vernix, scrubbing off evidence of our natality. We may prefer not to think much of our nakedness but draw decent drapes around the fact of our own birth. Thinking our way back into high appreciation of birth might not start best with our own. At a little distance, humans can see this good that we have, still, in common, that we come not naked into the world but daubed with generosity from the body that gave us a body.

---

26. Richardson, *Maternal Imprint*.

Chapter 6

Never Done (Motherhood)

THE RULE FOR PICK-UP at my children's kindergarten was for parents to come on foot. Parents, that is, moms, parked in nearby lots and stood outside the release doors at the appointed hour. Standing around outside the doors of this north-of-Boston school, moms sorted themselves into tight social knots with their backs to me as they traded intel about what their kids would and wouldn't eat, about deals on kids' jeans at the mall, or about vacation plans for Columbus Day leaf-peeping in New Hampshire, the family off to Story Land.

I am tempted to tell the story of how I got out of ever taking my kids to Story Land, but it's only a good story if you feel the bind. What bind? If you like Story Land or if you have never felt bound to go, if Story Land is obviously too expensive or too tacky or not the kind of thing that People Like Us do, it's not much of a story. Parents who don't feel the bind can create an alternative narrative that cheerfully excludes Story Land. I never pulled off the cheerful part of the alternative narrative. On my kids' behalf, I regret that many features of their childhood got sorted into categories of fun things I refused. There was the category of things we wouldn't do because we couldn't afford them, and the category of things that were actually evil, but also the category of things so foreign to my sense of the way things should be that kids' efforts at translation failed. I can see how my children could misread those as all the same category, though I maintain that those were separate baskets.

From most vantage points in most of the world for most of history, the very prospect of raising kids in so safe and affluent a way looks ridiculously luxurious. Complaining about it may seem petty, as if anybody should care about flaws of middle-class American parenting. Middle-class fashions shape the rules of parenting for Americans at large, whether individuals embrace, resist, or amend them.

On children's behalf mothers often have to follow rules foreign to their own childhood. Some women manage easily but others flounder because expectations shift fast in national norms and regional variations, plus whatever sprouts from the individualism pressing kids' conformity. Becoming a mother can feel like arriving in a country whose language you speak but discover locals only use an incomprehensible dialect, when your kids' survival depends on your fluency. In spite of practice, the job may always feel like "parenting with an accent," to use Masha Rumer's fine phrase. It is unclear how American women qualify as good moms beyond loving kids with unconditional acceptance and obeying those rules. The kind of mother any American woman can be depends not only on her preferences or her unique kids, but what the culture around makes plausible and therefore necessary in her caretaking.[1]

A SHORT HISTORY OF AMERICAN MOTHERHOOD

It wasn't always apple pie. American motherhood showed plenty of variations by region and race. In early years, in colonies where life was nasty, poor, and brutish, motherhood may have been too. Slavery undermined motherhood in a system that framed family life as reproduction of labor. New England settlements gave women sizable roles as deputy husbands and children's first teachers in small households and farmsteads. In the new days of American nationhood in the early nineteenth century, the ideology that historians call "Republican Motherhood" recreated the job, with women to raise sober, virtuous citizens. Victorian ideals presented mother as the sweet center of the home, the gentle caretaker who won her children's loyalties and discipline by silken cords of affection, what kids later would damn as guilt-tripping. Nineteenth-century white women having fewer children were able and expected to devote more attention and nurture to each one. Immigrant mothers and Black women had fewer opportunities to play this domestic role. The capable woman of the Progressive era was supposed to use her feminine influence for the common good, calling for

---

1. Rumer, *Parenting with an Accent*.

pure-food regulation and just tax schemes, her social role an extension of her mothering duties from private into public spheres.²

The Victorian matron got worn out in the early twentieth century. New-style modern mothers were more likely to follow advice given by experts stamped with scientific approval. In his 1894 guide, *The Care and Feeding of Children*, Dr. Luther Emmett Holt advised women to put children on schedules, to act more businesslike and efficient with them. Infatuation with efficiency motivated Frank and Lillian Gilbreth, whose household engineering inspired screen depictions of their Cheaper-by-the-Dozen project. The Gilbreths thought that education, discipline, and chores could be rationalized like factory work, subjected to time-and-motion studies and then optimized in every home. As Lillian's obituary reported, "when there was an unusual household task to be performed, the Gilbreths awarded the job, with pay, to the child who submitted the lowest bid."³

In the 1930s, deprivation and shared sacrifice refreshed appreciation for maternal self-giving. But mid-century America was not kind to mothers. Freudian analysis pounded a steady drumbeat bashing the damage inflicted by motherlove. Philip Wylie nastily impugned the smothering, psychosis-inducing nurture by moms that putatively emasculated sons and bred incompetence. Leo Kanner and Bruno Bettelheim faulted women in seemingly opposite terms, not for overmuch sentimentality but for their coolness, claiming that "refrigerator mothers," icy to their offspring, caused autism. Wylies critique echoed through laments during World War II and after, that America's young men were subpar in mental and physical health because of their mothers, a critique picked up with a twist by Betty Friedan. Friedan's *The Feminine Mystique* urged women not to be sucked in by pleasures of family and instead to use their talents in employment, energizing her call to arms in part by repeating accusations like Wylie's about the effects of attentive mothering.⁴

But what was the Baby Boom except a call to attentive mothering? Mid-twentieth-century women who shifted away from wartime occupations were bidden to find fulfillment in homemaking. In the 1970s, Adrienne Rich identified the problem as a conflict between motherhood as an experience and as an institution. The former could be amazing but the latter

2. Ulrich, *Goodwives*; Kerber, *Women of the Republic*; Koven and Michel, *Mothers of a New World*.

3. Apple, *Perfect Motherhood*; Crebs, "Family and Career."

4. This section relies on Plant, *Mom*, and Vandenberg-Daves, *Modern Motherhood*.

was lousy. Dr. Benjamin Spock's parenting manual encouraged women to trust their instincts even as it corrected them. This period of comparative freedom for moms and kids later was romanticized as something named free-range parenting by twenty-first-century moms who wished they were not expected to go to their kids' every ballet recital and soccer game. When women later went to work in greater numbers, quality time and having it all had to substitute for the mid-century arrangements.[5]

Free-range nostalgia came in part as protest against the dominant model for early twenty-first century, well-resourced middle-class parents, the approach named intensive parenting. One practical argument for intensive parenting was stranger danger, fear spawned by rare but well-publicized child kidnappings that made constant supervision seem necessary. One principled argument justifying intensive parenting was economic insecurity. Meritocracy's winners use the high-touch approach in hopes of securing similar spots for their children in a changing society with changing economic options. The logic is that because you do not know what kids' future jobs will be, you have to give them lots of opportunities. As soon as cultural arbiters became self-aware enough about this kind of childrearing to name it, intensive parenting drew disapproval even while continuing apace. Intensive parenting puts pressure on moms to feel bound to do all kinds of extraneous stuff for children and to think they should love doing it. This parenting style persuaded late twentieth-century women who had stepped away from jobs that their redirected creative energies were best devoted not to being something so retrograde as a housewife but to being a mom. When parenting fashions turned, moms who got good at this were faulted for it.[6]

MOTHERHOOD IN LIVED EXPERIENCE

In each cultural shift in parenting styles, mothers were punished by the new fad's authorities for obeying the dictates of the last era. Mothers were accused in turn of screwing up their children by being both too attentive and too distant. Victorian matrons were faulted for smother-love. Their successors, successful in scheduling and rationalizing rearing, were slammed

---

5. Rich, *Of Woman Born*; Skenazy, *Free-Range Kids*.

6. Annette Lareau introduced the phrase "concerted cultivation" in *Unequal Childhoods*. See also Zelizer, *Pricing the Priceless Child*; Senior, *All Joy and No Fun*; Warner, *Perfect Madness*; Pinsker, "'Intensive' Parenting Is Now the Norm in America."

for chilly rigidity. Spock-influenced moms were criticized for breeding entitled brats. In my children's young years, parents were supposed to play and praise. A decade or so later this cluster of behaviors was damned as helicopter parenting. Maybe some parents really did hover and bulldoze, but it didn't look like that at the time. Moms were doing what they were told they had to do. Shaming moms for being successful at intensive mothering is worse than having told them to do all that stuff in the first place. All the playground insults heaped on American mothers by the time I took my turn—viper mother, helicopter mother, tiger mother, free-range mother— suggest that there is no such thing as a good one.

Was my grandmother a good mother to mine? I don't think it would have occurred to either of them to pose that question. Of course she was a good mother. She took care of her five children. She taught them how to live. She connected them to their broader kin, she honored her husband and then the memory of him. I have no idea how her day-to-day self was with her children. Happy as a lark is how my mother described her childhood, surrounded by siblings who went to school and played together when they were not helping with the work of the house or visiting the extended family in Ohio.

My mother grew up capable and sociable. Then she had five children of her own, the number of cesarean births she could stand. Mothering us meant exposing us to the good things available where we lived, setting rules, enforcing manners, expecting good school performance, teaching us how to function while living in camaraderie in the meanwhile. I grew up thinking that five children was the right number and that people who did not reach this might be still working on it.

The parts of our lives that that my mother took care of were feeding us, teaching us household skills, telling us Christianity was true and Catholic practice was how you lived into it, taking us to playgrounds and hosting birthday parties, teaching us how to drive, teaching us about sex and drugs ("If somebody says to you, 'Hey kid, get in my car, I'll give you some candy,' and then hands you drugs, you say, 'No, I can't, my mother wouldn't let me.'"). In many parts of our childhood lives she did not much involve herself, for instance, in our friendships or socializing with our friends' parents, in schoolwork, in keeping up with popular culture, in advising on wardrobes. Many items on current lists of parental tasks she simply did not do. This is not a criticism. This was how the job was described to women then and socially enforced at the time. No one expected parents to supervise homework, help with homework, sign off on homework.

Sometimes retrospectives of 1970s motherhood are spoken in an uphill-both-ways idiom, as though motherhood was easier and childhood was harder then. Others think maybe childhood was better then, as free-range parenting advocates insist. In those years, moms got away with stowing toddlers in playpens to have free hands for a cigarette; in summer kids went biking around neighborhoods dawn to dusk until the dinner bell. Fans of this fantasy sometimes overlook its infrastructure, especially the presence of other moms in all those windows that were biked past, moms doing things like cooking the dinner for which the bell eventually would be rung. Kids may have had long summer bike-roaming hours, but they also had chores to do and siblings to mind.

My mother enabled learning and amusements but usually did not play board games, build snow forts, or color with us. She wove countless gestures of recognition into ordinary days. She operated within parenting conventions of the seventies and eighties in our upstate New York college town. She was also a little bit outside of them since she was from someplace else and divorced. At the time that seemed to reduce our opportunities but in the long run it probably expanded them. The times, plus her general savvy, plus our status as a "broken" family with a "single mother," left Mother a tiny bit susceptible to parenting advice that she otherwise may have brushed off. The same crowds buffing the stigma from divorce tried to teach those parents (since they were without partners) how to deal with kids in up-to-date ways, how to get in touch with their feelings and help kids get in touch with theirs. This gospel came to us occasionally on the record player in the spunky voice of Marlo Thomas teaching us we were "Free to Be You and Me," a plug for empathy that my mother really didn't need.[7]

My mother presupposed our obedience and respect and repaid that with selective disrespect to any other authority that might stand in the way of our flourishing, protesting busywork given by teachers, standing athwart the jaws of hell to rescue any who went astray. She left us to our own sibling tribes, which rotated around my two older sisters and sometimes functioned like the *Lord of the Flies* island but for that same reason was the tightest first society for each of us. She demonstrated astonishing nerve and perseverance in the face of adversity because adversity had a

---

7. Thomas et al., *Free to Be.*

face, who called her a dirtyrottensonofabitch to her face. That would be my father speaking. Other punier adversaries therefore were no contest for her.

One night a week or so Mother went to choir practice. I hated for her to go. Choir mostly met in winter and when she came home from practice, she usually came into our rooms to say good night to us, her face radiating that lovely scent we called The Cold Smell, which my siblings, all scientists, have never been able to explain by its chemistry. That was the other piece of her motherhood: my mother just was good to be around. She was funny and quick-thinking and flexible and resourceful. That was the model I had of motherhood, what you do as a mother. You are yourself, whose job it is to grow up your children and contend with whatever threatens them.

When I was in second grade my mother herniated some disks in her back and spent months lying on her bedroom floor on a mattress in excruciating pain. We brought her food and helped her get things. Nursing her while she was recuperating—that plus *excruciating* were words I was proud to know as an eight-year-old—was tedious work. I brought tea and toast and took away the plates but then she might say, the floor is so dusty, can you sweep it? The floor did not look dusty to me, as I told her. When I'm lying here all day flat on my back, she replied, I am looking right at the dusty floor, it's dusty, can you sweep it? I swept. I often was crabby about sweeping and caretaking. Late in the afternoons my younger brother would materialize, after baseball practice or basketball practice or coming in from building forts out of sticks or damming creeks, smelling of the fresh world outdoors. He would come in to visit my mother and sit on the edge of the mattress to talk to her. And she would say, it's so nice to have you help me when I'm lying here flat on my back.

Before I had kids I didn't worry whether I would be a good mom. You were a good mom if you passed along tradition, if you taught children requisite skills, and if you loved them. That first part has proven a stumbling block. Mothers come up short because kids may no longer inhabit tradition or live where mothers grew up, literally or metaphorically. So mothers must not only figure out how to do the new things but learn to act as though those things are natural. A mother wants to be able to do what her kids need her to do. Sometimes she can't because she figures out too late what they need or she does not have the right skills. I know how to do laundry and cook dinner and pack a beach bag and write research papers and thank-you notes. For my kids' sake I should have learned other skills, but I didn't know which ones in advance.

Disoriented

I never daydreamed about having babies. I didn't not want children, I just didn't fantasize about it. I assumed having children was something that usually came in adult life, to be planned *on* though not necessarily planned *for*. It seemed like one of those experiences in which people liked some parts better than others, but liking it was neither reason to do it nor not to do it. The idea behind the old Planned Parenthood nostrum, "every child a wanted child," miscasts the project of having children, though I see what point family-planners were trying to make. An expectant parent does not know what to want in a child, and even the most planned children may not turn out as wanted. If I ever thought dreamily about having children, it was picturing myself holding one by the hand to walk to the public library. I thought what you did with children was to present them with some good things in the world—playgrounds, books, ice-cream cones, art supplies.

Baby #1 knocked the wind out of me. Wow, she was beautiful and could not exhaust fascination. The new-baby sleep tax is brutal, but there was a short span between her colicky phase and sleep-training phase where she would slumber into morning past eight or so, during which time I could have pretended to be a normal person and have breakfast and read the newspaper. Instead, what I actually did was lurk by her room hoping she would wake up so I could be with her again. Afternoons at rest I propped her on the slope made by my knees and she stared at me, receptive and amazed, like the way we are supposed to look at God. I paid more attention to her than maybe was strictly necessary. I paid attention because she was so beautiful but also because I was trying to do the right thing, what guidebooks told me, to respond to different cries for food or a diaper change or stimulation.

Thinking about what was in my baby's head made me wonder how anything gets in anyone's head. How absurd it is that care for children is understood as drudge work. The work is way above us and too hard. All my babies were pretty easy according to the standards books apply. All three ate well, slept well, and transitioned smoothly out of diapers. Not one of them ever stuck a bead up her nose or a finger in an electrical socket or jumped from the top bunk. Still, at the time, taking care of babies felt impossibly hard. One time a nurse made a courtesy visit to our house to see how everything was going. She told me she was there to check on my breastfeeding, was it okay? Breastfeeding was fine. I was amazed that my body could present itself as food. It was everything else that I was failing at.

Never Done (Motherhood)

The experience of new motherhood leaves little original to say. It is trite and worse to describe the drunk love of loving a newborn. Everybody knows about that. I saw on my baby all those attributes that other people tell new mothers to notice: soft hair, soft skin, warm sweet scent, the exaggerated pucker of the mouth, the toes like tiny peas. But having the usual response doesn't mean that it's not a revelation. I held her whole being in the world on the weight of one arm while she nursed and I stared down at her face, a face I came to know better than I knew any other face at the time, even my own. I started seeing people differently in line at the grocery store, wondering how much more honor they deserved from me than I usually gave them since someone some time had looked so long at them like that when they were new and milk-fed. And what if no one ever had looked at them that way? Then they deserved even more care. All faces deserve that delight in being beheld, but most beholders cannot see what should be seen. One gift of being mother or father is awareness, through practice, of how good that face is.

The effort expended in meeting the bodily needs of a small human is not the same as effort called forth in enjoying their company. Children require so much physical care: cleaning, diapering, nose-wiping, sliding their arms into sleeves and their sleeves into coats, tying shoes, cutting fruit, squeezing toothpaste, lifting in and out of beds and seats and cars, opening doors, opening boxes, picking up toys. They get hungry and need food. Whether in affluence or poverty, providing food is a task mothers manage almost round the clock—getting it, anticipating kids' want of it, preparing it, the fiddling of sippy-cup valves and filling the cup and closing the cup, and then cleaning up after the event of eating, disorder generated all out of proportion with quantities of food eaten. Clothes too demand effort out of proportion with size, fixing each snap, button, tooth of zipper track, pressing limbs into pants, pressing thumbs into mittens, heels into boots, jimmying swimsuits onto and wet off of impatient bodies. Bathing and brushing teeth and brushing hair and helping into highchair and car seat and bed, and then out, and then in again. Then parents teach them how to do all these things on their own, which is more work than doing it for them. Play means scattering things on the floor. It's tempting to see the problem with American childrearing as a problem of affluence, that we just have so much stuff that we have to spend lots of time cleaning it and putting it away. We do make things harder. But wealth doesn't create the mess. The mess comes from embodiment. The mother's body gives birth to a body that no longer gets warmth, food, or shelter automatically without requesting it but still wants all those and has to feel the need before getting it met. Felt needs hurt more and get said louder. Of course, someone else can do this physical care work for money rather than love. Parents can express love also by paying others to provide care. We hope love stays in it somewhere, though that is a lot to try to buy through an hourly wage.

Much of the work of childrearing is the work of caring for the body, a fact which might be obvious but was a revelation to me. If the task of growing up is in some respects to turn the body inside out, to coax the inner person to govern the outer one, childhood reveals humans to be something else than rational creatures. I hankered to be more than the tender of the needs of bodies, though tending to bodily needs is the way to love children. My toddlers bloomed under tending—the one who noticed the world and narrated it; the one who shone with pleasure and radiated it; the one born with rhythm, who pulled himself up and clung to the edge of a table and moved to the beat of music before he could stand alone on his feet.

My first baby had such interesting ideas and we had such interesting conversations before she learned to talk. Then for a while I felt shortchanged, her monosyllables a regression. The disappointment was brief. She was telling me paragraphs when she was two. Some of her baby speech is lost forever because I never understood it before she outgrew it and she forgot what she meant. She was generous with her younger siblings this way, translating their baby speech so that we could understand it before those words disappeared: emmalow meant animal, ga-ga-ga-ga meant car transporter, truck-inside meant construction site. Mothers can observe children at close enough range to gather and preserve this knowledge. They can save the artifacts of babyhood to pass along to children a self that the children themselves do not remember. Grown children may find this embarrassing. Mothers may be loyal to children's discarded loves. Sometimes parents see the value of those old things more than children do themselves, even later.

For some things, like Barbies, I had a policy in place before reckoning came due. But I screwed up Santa. The first time someone asked my firstborn, "Was Santa good to you?" I saw my mistake. I disliked the elaborate deception of Santa Claus worldbuilding and all its phases and recalibrations, how Santa could be in many places at once or could fit in architecturally unsuitable spaces. I had Christian friends explain that Santa-belief is propaedeutic to the gospel. I was not persuaded. I got defter at playing along about Santa after my first child, but for a while my kids believed Santa was real and he came to everybody's house except theirs. I am sorry for that.

Barbie and Santa Claus and Disney characters were ever popping out from behind corners to remind me that raising children depends on the place where you are. To be sure, within one's own four walls one can, within limits, adopt countercultural ways, but at a price one's children may not be able to afford. I scrupled, for instance, against buying plastic water bottles, back when it seemed unbelievable that in a country with basically safe water supply it would be normal to prefer getting water in single-use plastic bottles. Moms who came for playdates demonstrated this was not acceptable and their kids wouldn't drink from our tap—strange in hindsight, given how eco-conscious our neighborhood was supposed to be. Or, I did not realize that middle schools require uniforms, and I should have given my daughter the popular garments she wanted instead of a lecture on the errors of branding, though I still think that lecture is valid.

Nice relatives got into habits of giving my first child educational toys rather than the regular kind because they assumed I would want this. Some of those were good gifts. All three children brought big imagination to small toys. Felt and wood and interlocking bricks and plastic houses for tiny people were materials for them to make a world. They showed what they were thinking through what they drew and built. Some days, most days, first with my eldest, I got on the floor to play with them and watch them play. This is the style of mothering my maternity was born into. I did activities with my children because they were what seemed appropriate and what other moms in the pediatricians' office did and what the pediatrician assumed I was doing.

But that thing, getting on the floor with children to play with them all the time, turned out to be the hallmark and cardinal sin of parenting in the late 1990s, the thing shortly after lambasted and pilloried. I did it unreflectively, unaware that I was choosing to sit on the floor with little play people because people like me were nudged to do it. It felt natural to pay attention to my children because they were so interesting. Even so, I knew how costly this was, squandering time when children were occupied and had no bodily needs or dangers. Since then, when I have seen other women with young children, the danger of this floor-playing habit has seemed so glaring that I have wanted to take them by the shoulders and warn them, look! Don't do that! Kids don't need you to play with them all the time!

Playing with kids all the time is not a natural thing but a culturally specific American practice supported by anxiety about work-life balance!

That's true. And yet. I played with my kids because it was the rightest thing in the world to do that. I could do it and they wanted me to. I taught them things and they received my words and they were good company. It was a pleasure—the pleasure of their being—to sit with them in activities, to build things that turned into inside jokes, to watch them discover the world. That time spent on the floor was some of the most valuable time I spent in my life, time not to be made up in their lives later or substituted for by anything else. Spending a lot of time allowed for the particulars that made it good, time to learn the vocabulary of children's interior world.[8]

When my eldest was about a year old she smelled a flower. I had leaned over to put my nose in a flower. She watched me do it and then leaned over and put her nose in the flower. She inhaled. Maybe I said after that, "We're smelling the flowers," or "That's a flower, doesn't it smell nice?" That is the gloria-in-excelsis part of childrearing. Good things get shaken visible when a parent directs time and attention to another's encounter with the world, and when the other allows this observation because of returned love and trust built through time. Mutual focus enables a care hard to come by any other way. Mothering came studded with some sparkling bits.

But large swaths of childrearing are not fun. Having children because it seems fun is not an ideal reason to do it. Dwindling birthrates in the twenty-first century reveal what a terrible miscalculation it was to lead on adults by promising that motherhood is fun. If you have children because you expect them to be fun, you have to find stamina somewhere else for the body labor and emotional strain and distraction that rearing entails, especially the kind that comes years after the baby phase.

That thing that virtue ethicists and grandmothers say, that you don't know what you're made of until challenge comes, mothers discover that at 2 AM feedings after 10 PM crying jags, at everything soaked through, the diaper and the onesie and the pajamas and the blanket and the crib sheet. They discover it at breakfast the next morning with the other kids, or in the car on the way to school with other mothers watching. A mother-to-be can work on herself beforehand but the actual job that her motherhood will be does not exist until it is hers. The problem of motherhood is not just how much a mother has to teach kids, how to preheat the oven for baking

---

8. De Marneffe anatomizes the complexity of enjoying motherhood in *Maternal Desire*.

cookies, how to quit a job or file taxes, how to fasten a bra, how to use a semicolon. The problem is that the person showing up for them is you. The hard thing about motherhood was that I had to be the one showing up for it, sack that I am of anxieties and selfishness and flubbed ambitions of magnanimity. A mother not only must do certain things but also be a certain kind of person. If things all go as intended, mothers turn into a different kind of person, one interrupted, like a survivor in wartime or a Shakespearean fool. Mothers become the kind of person who meet absurdity as normalcy because there is so much absurdity all the time and they must pretend that it is unremarkable. They must turn into persons who have to traffic in the tragicomic and the bureaucratic and the brute physical, sunup to sundown, then get up and do it again. Motherhood is full-body transformation that some call matrescence, no less discombobulating than adolescence.[9]

Strangely—or maybe not strangely—the parenting style that prioritized mothers' close attention to kids' enjoyment bred some frustration. One July morning at a playground with kindergarten kids and their moms, when it came time to take kids home for lunch and naps, I saw one woman high-five others and say, "Whew! Another summer day, down!" Until then I did not know I was supposed to be relieved how fast summer days fly by.

WHAT'S STRANGE ABOUT AMERICAN MOTHERHOOD

The job description of childrearing was under review while I had my first baby. I had no idea. Motherhood and fatherhood both were taking strange new shape when my kids came around. The new fatherhood developed in the 1990s was supposed to update the old kind, men serving not only as breadwinners but changing diapers and being fun. Some commentators spurned the new fatherhood, proposing that fathers who supported their kids by working for a paycheck already were doing plenty to live into their office. But since the end of the twentieth century, fathers were supposed to start doing what mothers did because mothers had already begun doing what fathers did. Nurture and breadwinning could be shared by both parents. Soon enough it seemed useful to describe generically what both parents were doing as "parenting."[10]

---

9. Jones, *Matrescence*.

10. Gilbert Meilaender hesitated at this shift in "The New Fatherhood." See recent examples of new fatherhood in Marche, *Unmade Bed*, and Gessen, *Raising Raffi*.

Maybe the activity needed the new ungendered name since "to mother" a child suggests a kind of tea-and-blanket nurture and "to father" a child connotes the act that fertilized the egg. The term *parenting* has some benefits, framing what is done on children's behalf as shared by both people (or whomever, or however many) rather than sorting duties into mom-and-pop ones. The term also makes the tasks sound more official, a promotion via relabeling. But it is a poor turn to make that noun into a verb, to parent instead of to be a parent. Childrearing is a better term if an ungendered one must be found for adults' nurture of their little people.

There are lots of other ways of raising children than the twenty-first-century American one. But there aren't many plausible ways as long as you raise them here. You aren't really bringing up bébé if you aren't in France. When American parents covet somebody else's childrearing manners, whether the Parisian rule that no toddlers interfere with cocktail hour or Almanzo Wilder, in the *Little House on the Prairie* series, waiting patiently to be served last at breakfast, no genius hack can be imported to solve our problems. For many of us, parenting problems are a function of social mobility, egalitarian manners, and democracy. American rags-to-riches stories presuppose parents still in rags or dead. Otherwise what would it mean for characters to grow up to be something special and different? A friend with a happy childhood and nice parents once told me that as a kid, she loved to read books about orphaned children who made clever homes for themselves in cozy places like old train cars, except that she wanted the parents not to be dead. She liked the idea of playing make-believe in a boxcar but would rather head home when dinnertime rolled around. That hybrid resembles the regnant ideal in my kids' middle-class comfortable childhood: be whatever you want to be while your parents support the make-believe. American children are supposed to move in circles their parents never entered. We love it that way, the American dream. What that means is that mothers may find themselves almost constantly swimming up streams on children's behalf that they never crossed themselves.[11]

Philosopher Agnes Callard faults an aspect of this rigamarole, what she calls acceptance parenting. Acceptance parenting demands that moms and dads commit in advance to accepting whatever kids decide to do, a commitment made not only to children in their activities and academics but to their self-made identities. Twenty-first-century parents are supposed to be so pre-committed that they hardly are aware of having contorted

---

11. Druckerman, *Bringing up Bébé*; Wilder, *Farmer Boy*.

themselves into this posture. Indeed, they may only become aware when some old impulse to judge momentarily blocks their child's self-expression, at which point the ashamed parents scramble backward to affirm the child after all. Parents' chief task now appears to be providing moral and material support for kids' self-creation, not seldom committing their resources to kids' subversion of the very principles parents wanted to uphold.[12]

Twenty-first-century parenting culture made moms handmaidens to children's self-definition. Unbelievably, in the 2020s, even as the outer frameworks of parenting have shifted from free-range to intensive and back, advice givers still obligate parents to facilitate kids' liberation, to let kids be themselves and get out of the way, as though inventing a new commandment. Intensive-parenting moms keep getting invited to sign up for, to supply costumes and snacks for, kids' self-defining experiences. Mothers have been invited to create the world that children want—Girl Scout Cookie Mom! Book Fair Volunteer! Field Day Referee!—and then erase themselves. It is a mistake to read the activity-festooned world of fun and deluxe experiences as just the sin of intense parents' overinvolvement. Kids of a certain stratum want that stuff, are culturally bidden to demand it in order to be anything they want to be. Of course kids cannot be whatever they want, mine or yours. Lots of things kids might want to be are not worth being. Some things worth being are hard to name winningly to young children looking for a label to grow into. Social expectations of childhood shape job descriptions for motherhood. By the twenty-first century's second decade, those expectations reframed motherhood as a dud job, testified by overwhelmed-mom memoirs and mom-rage writing.

What's strange about motherhood is that conversation about it tends to shift weight from parents to children and back again, women's ambitions to be a good mom refitted to satisfaction as good-enough one. Most things written about motherhood conceal something. Like other jobs, you usually don't write your own ticket. Mommy lit bewails how hard parenting is. The motherhood plot is a story of retrieving oneself after overcoming the startling obstacles of having a baby so that the protagonist can return to being herself, which is a self defined by whatever she does for work and fun. Usually writers also let slip somewhere that their own babies are gorgeous and interesting, and that the solution is finding good daycare or egalitarian spouse or both.[13]

12. Callard, "Acceptance Parenting."
13. British psychologist Donald Winnicott coined the term "good-enough mother."

BETTER THINKING ABOUT MOTHERHOOD

The motherhood that raised me seemed to solve many problems people perennially confront. Women got the choice to raise children or do something else. More women got resources to make raising children enjoyable and could count on a spouse as full-fledged co-parent from cradle to graduation. Instead emphasis fell wrong in each category. Once every child is a choice, women have had to justify the choice against other ambitions or others' ambitions for this mortal life, often justifying it on grounds of enjoyment. Taking care of kids entails much that is not so enjoyable to do, and co-parenting slides into fights over fairness and toil. Leaning the other way receives kids as gifts consequent to embodied love, eternal-souled companions in common life.

Platitudes pretend motherhood is all sweet. Mommy-lit retrenchment complaints can be just as false to experience. Books recognizing that childrearing can be hard are right until they slide into the genre of horror story. Horror may seem the right genre to some who were but recently on the receiving end of acceptance parenting and who had not envisioned what the arrangement would mean for them as parents. It may seem horrible because formative years for young women so aggressively bifurcate family and career ambition, and because parenting fashions emphasize autonomy. Envisioning motherhood as not horror is urgent now that politics and culture and sometimes the earth itself seem conspired against the prospect of childbearing.[14]

One kind of childrearing advice speaks down from the pedestal of science, using biology and psychology to explain what children *are*, sometimes without self-awareness that society shapes behavior. Pediatricians often direct parents this way. The deal that scientific experts offer parents is that if they do *this*, kids will do *that*. Parents who are obedient in following rules may think that following best-practice rules would yield good results, would habituate children to grow into good behavior. I thought so. Then the paradigm shifted. About the time when my eldest reached double digits, the epithet "frontal lobe" began to slither through school pick-up line gossip. I first heard this theory from a serious person, my female OB-GYN,

---

For a recent writer coming to terms with baby care, see O'Connell, *And Now We Have Everything*.

14. Examples presenting motherhood as horror story include Cusk, *Life's Work*; Molnar, *Nursery*; Chan, *School for Good Mothers*; See also Adamy, "Why Americans Are Having Fewer Babies."

who tried to pass pleasantries while my legs were in stirrups, explaining her own son's misadventures in terms of his undeveloped executive functioning. This theory proposes that kids cannot be held responsible because their brains do not gel sufficiently until age twenty-five. Their brains are like toddler brains again, my gynecologist said, demolishing parents' decade-plus labor of habituation with words more chilling than her speculum. Of course serious people could not actually believe this, I thought as I got off the table, because otherwise we would not let fifteen-year-olds drive cars.

The long reach of science notwithstanding, its dicta have had less influence on childhood in the last few decades than ones from intensive parenting. Too often analyses applied to realms of mothers and children talk past each other, as though of one set of recommendations had no implications for the other. Intensive parenting focuses on the quality of children's experience and the reverse is true for public conversation about childcare arrangements. For sure, safe, high-quality childcare is a broad desideratum. Often it is hard to tell what that thing looks like from a child's point of view. Do they like it? What difference does it make if they don't? Though any particular daycare might be great and kids flourish there, it is bracing how little of children's actual experience figures into conversations about childcare.

Addressing a family's common good invites looking beyond it for help. For a period, during an early 1990s round of battles over definitions of the family, "It Takes a Village" was the rallying cry of one faction whose titular head was Hillary Clinton. Wife of one presidential candidate and then a candidate herself, Clinton insisted that raising children takes more than just two parents, it takes a whole community, that so-called village. It does. But many of us don't have a village. The state is not a village. Individual moms can overcome some of the isolation of at-home childrearing by piecing together carpools and playgroups. But building those networks can be as hard as making friends in middle school, and with much higher stakes. Not all mothers can invent villages. Do the other mothers at the playground like you? Do their kids like your kid?[15]

Around Mother's Day each year, critics complain that caregiving is devalued. It is. Setting a price, though, suggests that everything has a price. Rethinking that price requires rethinking family life. Some time between my 1970s childhood and twenty-first-century parenthood, public language about the family got weird. Family sometimes got hyped as family values or celebrated for diverse shapes of fictive-elective kin. Rethinking family life

15. Clinton, *It Takes a Village*.

should acknowledge a common good beyond the good of each individual member. Then others outside the family should be called upon to support the dependencies within it. Society owes honor to mothers in the form of recognition and not only a holiday or subsidy. Since caring for a dependent can make the caregiver herself dependent, Eva Feder Kittay advises that, "When we respect an individual as some mother's child, we honor the efforts of that mothering person and symbolically of all mothering persons."[16]

It can be excruciatingly difficult, excruciating and difficult, to do this job even at a mediocre level. It is easier if everything goes well for one's children, though for most children at least something does not go well. Part of motherhood is trying to move oneself around the great suffering of one's beloved, taking into one's body the sufferings of one who came out of one's body. When the world inflicts injuries on children, mothers feel the hurts too. Motherhood sticks in our faces the incommensurateness of us all, our insufficiency for each other, our desire for others' good, our causing harm by trying to help.[17]

Taking care of children names more than a generic set of tasks, that gerund "parenting." One person's experience of rearing children can be totally different from others'. The job of motherhood under varied conditions might be better managed with a trick from the toolkit of Peg Bracken. Bracken's 1960s *I Hate to Cook Book* began with aghast astonishment at how hard cooking for a family was and how much it interfered with the other things women were supposed to be doing for their families. Her solutions conceded neither to perfectionist standards nor to flat failure, and certainly not to teeth-gnashing.[18]

We could do with a new book of that kind about the tasks of motherhood. The book a latter-day Bracken might write, in this era of ambivalence and low birthrates, would not be called "I Hate Being a Mom" or "I Hate Children." Maybe it could be called, "I Hate Dance Recitals," or "I Hate to Fill Out the FAFSA," or "I Love when One Child Unwraps a Band-Aid for His Brother." The right book would cut through the agglomerations of childhood entitlements stuck on by the market and status anxiety. Mothers should be free to affirm that both extremes can be true about raising even average children: that you should glory in the miraculous presence of small humans who bloom like sunflowers under your gaze and make you actually

---

16. Kittay, *Love's Labor*, 74; Sargeant, *Dignity of Dependence*.
17. Elkins, *Mary, Mother of Martyrs*.
18. Bracken, *I Hate to Cook Book*.

Never Done (Motherhood)

feel more like the sun, and also admit the tedium and pain of caring for beloved embodied creatures. That kind of book could affirm the great good of raising human life and steel parents for the hard parts.

Chapter 7

Be Not Afraid (Faith)

IN LATE SUMMER AFTERNOONS when we were at my grandmother's house, Baba turned on the rosary. My mother called us and we gathered around the couch in the living room. My siblings and I usually did not pray the rosary the rest of the year at home. The rosary was prayed on our knees with elbows leaning on the cushions of the couch or the armchairs. The rosary is a Catholic devotion that groups prayers into sections, five decades—packages of ten—grouped into Mysteries, the Sorrowful Mysteries, the Joyful Mysteries, the Glorious Mysteries, which all ends up with a Salve Regina. Some people use beads to help keep track. I knew most of the rosary's parts separately, the Our Father (what I later learned Protestants call the Lord's Prayer) and Hail Mary (which Protestants omit).

A family praying together around the living room, that was what the pioneers of radio rosary intended. Pittsburgh is an important city in the history of radio, its KDKA the first licensed commercial radio station in the United States. In other radio-rich, Catholic-heavy parts of the United States, Slavs got to hear the rosary in their own language, making it normal for Catholics to do in their living rooms just what we were doing in those Pittsburgh summers. Of course the rosary came before the radio. Christians combined prayers into this form a long time ago. Nineteenth- and twentieth-century Catholics were energized to pray the rosary after apparitions of the Virgin Mary implored children in Fatima and Lourdes to do so. In my grandmother's living room, we were glad we had the religious freedom to pray the rosary. In Cold War America, the rosary was not just directed to God and Mary but against secularization and the tyrannies of the age. To us, that meant Russia.

BE NOT AFRAID (FAITH)

I don't think my siblings were super motivated to pray the rosary but I also don't think it ever occurred to us, not to me anyway, not to do it. Sometimes the torpor of humid afternoons made any scheduled thing desirable, and this was what was scheduled. That is not to say my mind was always in it. It was hard to pay attention. Maybe doing was the point, being on my knees and trying. The good thing about the rosary is that it goes on and on. Maybe some people who pray it are fully attentive so that every time they say, "thy will be done," they absolutely mean it every time. Maybe for them repetition only adds emphasis, *thy will be done*. For me repetition allowed catching up. When my mind wandered on one Glory Be, I could swing the brain around to catch it the next time. The rosary draws praying people into eternity playing on a loop, outside of ordinary time. This loop of heavenly time could be broken in two ways in Pittsburgh summers. The regular way came from inside the eternal loop itself, the Salve Regina, our signal that the cycle was drawing to a close.

The other way eternal time got broken up came from outside, right outside the window. Sometimes over the dolorous voice from the radio, calliope music rang from the street. My brothers and sisters and I kept up with Hail Marys while a song outside slowed and sped and paused louder again right in front of the house. Whoever was kneeling against the couch could look out the window to see the ice cream truck, painted with the smiling face of the Good Humor Man gesturing at his favorite frozen confections. The truck came practically close enough to touch. We almost never could touch it because we could not move until the rosary was over. Even then, we would not have ice cream before dinner, and dinner came right after rosary. The ice cream truck was a city thing. We did not have a vehicle like this on our street in Ithaca, a truck that brought the treat to you and offered choices, so that each child could each have something different and not only as a function of popsicle-box randomness. We loved the ice cream truck, craved it, and on summer afternoons at Baba's, heard it stop and drive away.

A SHORT HISTORY OF AMERICAN CHRISTIANITY WILL NEVER SUFFICE

This short history of being Christian in America is riskier than the other short histories in this book because so much is at stake. I repent of omissions and commissions in telling it. Christianity layered atop Indigenous religions and has come here in many varieties. America is not a Christian nation, though there have been many kinds of Christians here.[1]

In the beginning was the Word. Christianity professes that Jesus is fully human and also fully divine in a formulation hashed out amid imperial and ecclesiastical politics in the early centuries of the church. The Roman Catholic Church maintains that the bread and wine at the Eucharist are both real bread and wine and also the real presence of the body and blood of Jesus, in a formulation hashed out by St. Thomas Aquinas.[2]

In the beginning of Christian histories of America usually come the pilgrims to Plymouth, Massachusetts, in the 1620s. A decade later their broad-shouldered brethren appear in the Massachusetts Bay Colony. But way before that, at the sixteenth century's dawn, Spanish Catholics came exploring and conquering in the south and the west of what became the United States. Christianity in the United States was Catholic before it was Protestant, competing empires replanting institutions and animosities from the old world. The Spanish wiped out French Protestants who tried to find some respite from persecution by settling in Florida in the 1560s. Christian missionaries of all varieties evangelized and baptized some Indigenous people they encountered, people who also were enslaved, murdered, and dispossessed by settlers.[3]

America was not founded as a beacon of religious freedom, although toleration and liberty took root so deeply that people sometimes mistake them as native species. New England offered some haven to religious dissenters. For the most part, those settlers' goal was not freedom for everybody to worship as conscience dictated, but to reconstruct the church as they would have done in their home country if permitted. Roger Williams did embrace religious freedom in Rhode Island and William Penn did in Pennsylvania. The new nation wrote religious freedom into its Constitution, though church establishments survived for years in New England. American popular culture kept a Protestant hue longer still. Thomas Jefferson venerated religious freedom, won political allies among New England

---

1. Fea, *Was America Founded as a Christian Nation?*
2. Noll, Komline, and Kantzer Komline, *Turning Points*, 27–64.
3. Summaries in this history from Coffman, *Turning Points in American Church History*, here 11–29. See also Winship, *Godly Republicanism*, and Bayne, *Missions Begin with Blood*.

dissenters, and named farmers God's favorite people. Jefferson thought that before long Americans all would be Unitarians.⁴

Americans regularly displayed high expectations for God's extraordinary attention. John Winthrop told Massachusetts settlers that God gave them permission to draw up their own articles in covenant with him. English evangelist George Whitefield traveled thousands of miles back and forth across the Atlantic and the east coast, part of an Awakening in the eighteenth century, bringing the word of God to crowds from the late 1730s until his 1770 death, echoing the gospel so mightily that even notorious skeptic Benjamin Franklin plunked coins into the collection. Penitents at camp meetings in the nineteenth century met God's deliverance with whole-body responses: jumping, barking, falling down, crying out. Early nineteenth-century Christianity was democratized, Nathan Hatch demonstrates, and democratized Christianity allowed humbler people to redefine expressions of the faith. The resulting multiplicity meant that earnest believers could wonder which version of Christianity was right or wrong, a puzzle whose solution suggested that maybe all the sects were wrong, as Joseph Smith concluded. In the woods of upstate New York, Smith's seeking was rewarded in the 1820s by visions and a revelation inscribed on golden plates, entrusted to the Church of Jesus Christ of Latter-Day Saints. Many nineteenth-century Americans calculated that Jesus was coming back soon. William Miller and his followers expected the Lord to come in October 1844. They were disappointed.⁵

Some observers from overseas found this Christianity-from-the-bottom-up distasteful, even dangerous. Swiss-German theologian Philip Schaff rued that liberty enabled every "fanatic" who cooked up a new religious idea to build new churches in their own likeness. New sects could find followers by touting notions in a religious realm disturbingly like a marketplace, where "[e]very theological vagabond and peddler may drive here his bungling trade, without passport or license and sell his false ware at pleasure." In contrast, Alexis de Tocqueville was fascinated by the luxuriant, unruly growth of American Christianity. He offered the United States as evidence against philosophers who imagined that "religious zeal had to burn itself out as freedom and education increased." Contrary to patterns in

---

4. Coffman, *Turning Points*, 31–50; Jefferson, *Notes on the State of Virginia*, Query XIX.

5. Coffman, *Turning Points*, 71–90, 131–34, 149; Hatch, *Democratization of American Christianity*.

Europe, where secularization and progressive hostility were leveled against religion, the new nation's separation of church and state let "the spirit of religion" and "the spirit of freedom" stay "intimately linked together in joint reign over the same land."[6]

Revivals set hearts aflame with the love of God and split churches apart. Another Awakening, a second round in the nineteenth century, birthed reform movements like abolition, temperance, Sunday schools, missions. Christian churches wrangled over the issue of slavery. Though some mobilized sacred texts to defend slavery, enslaved people and free Blacks expressed their faith in forms that discarded those theological errors. The first African American church was founded in South Carolina in 1773. Faith and life in Black churches contributed profoundly to American Christian experience. Before the nation split in Civil War, American denominations split over slavery.[7]

In the late nineteenth century, many American believers demonstrated commitment to the gospel by taking it overseas. At home, Christians discovered the Holy Spirit also breathing new power into their churches. The 1906 revivals at the Azusa Street Church in Los Angeles included lively expressions of the gifts of the Holy Spirit, speaking in tongues and healings, creating Pentecostal and charismatic expressions that believers around the world would come to embrace. Twentieth-century churches split again in confrontations with modernity, especially over Scripture and evolution. Protestants arrayed themselves into tribes, modernists and fundamentalists, then mainline churches and evangelical ones. Those rearrangements also bred new fellowship among believers across denominations, so that being Methodist or Baptist or Episcopalian might come to seem less important than a right view of God's word and right stance on moral questions. During and after the World Wars, American Christians contended with the moral meaning of new world powers, Nazi Germany, the USSR, and communist China. Christianity mid-century also fueled movements for civil rights in the 1960s, Black churches and clergy building solidarity amid conflict and violence.[8]

---

6. Schaff quoted in Howard, *God and the Atlantic*, 17; Tocqueville, *Democracy in America*, 345.

7. Coffman, *Turning Points*, 72–91, 131–51; Harvey, *Through the Storm*; Noll, *Civil War*.

8. Coffman, *Turning Points*, 193–215, 23–256.

Be Not Afraid (Faith)

After the wars too, Americans began coming to Christ in novel, dramatic fashion by means of new mass-communications technologies, radio and television broadcasts, or full-stadium revival preaching. In the mainstream, a broad Protestantism blessed America during the 1950s under the presidency of Dwight Eisenhower, who inserted a line into the Pledge of Allegiance sticking the nation under God, and who imagined the American way of life as grounded in "a deeply felt religious faith, and I don't care what it is." Billy Graham told thousands of listeners attending his Crusades that they must be born again. Many were. Conversion could be a public affair or private one, mild or dramatic. Former hippies found the Lord in the 1970s in the Jesus movement.[9]

Smoothing sharp angles and blurring historic divisions, like-minded believers grouped together beyond old labels. Evangelical Christians, distinct from fundamentalists, became more self-aware if still hard to categorize. Exactly what constitutes an Evangelical continues to cause debate. David Bebbington categorizes Evangelicals by their emphases on conversion, the centrality of the Bible and the cross, plus commitment to activism, a formulation others amend by emphasizing individual assurance, affections, or mission. Holding to these principles in common allowed believers to minimize denominational differences and cultivate fellowship. Priority given to conversion, one's own and one's obligation to offer the gospel to others, cast Christianity in seeker-friendly terms.[10]

When Catholics flooded into the United States in the nineteenth century, many Protestants reviled them as superstitious drunkards and subjects of a foreign prince, the pope. Catholics settled in ethnic parishes and tried to maintain traditions, though assimilation was neither easy nor entirely desirable for many. Pope Leo XIII worried about US Catholics' drift down slopes greased by Protestants and condemned "Americanism" as heresy. Catholic life was transformed in the twentieth century with the Second Vatican Council.[11]

In the 1980s some Protestants and Catholics, for whom suspicion may have been the most charitable posture previously offered one another, became likelier to see each other as co-religionists as they joined in common

---

9. Coffman, *Turning Points*, 257–78; Douthat quotes Eisenhower's line as example of public piety paired with smugness and ignorance in *Bad Religion*, 52.

10. Coffman, *Turning Points*, 86–87; Noll, Bebbington, and Marsden, eds., *Evangelicals*.

11. Dolan, *American Catholic Experience*; O'Toole, *Faithful*.

cause around moral issues, especially abortion, sexual immorality, and aggressive secularism. An "ecumenism of the trenches" helped draw Evangelicals and Catholics together in the 1990s. The collaboration also had rougher edges. Sympathetic politicians, mostly Republicans, backed family values or Judeo-Christian values to build support among a group self-aware as a Moral Majority, as Rev. Jerry Falwell named his organization. Ties between the Republican party and Evangelicals grew tighter as candidates campaigned for faith and freedom. In the early twenty-first century, this movement seemed regnant, then chastened, then resurgent again by the 2016 election cycle when, gathering force with other right-leaning and anti-establishment groups, it set its blessing on Donald Trump.[12]

BELIEVING IN LIVED EXPERIENCE

Like America, the Christianity I had was Catholic before any Protestant kind took hold. I went to a Catholic church every Sunday as a child. My grandmother's Catholicism felt like something from a foreign country, which it was. It probably had seemed that way to her too at first, since it was not the way she worshiped when she was a child. In Czechoslovakia her family was Uniate, believers whose Eastern Rite liturgy and worship look like Orthodox Christianity but who are under papal authority due to political exigencies. When my grandmother came back to beautiful Ohio, without an Eastern Rite church nearby, the family worshiped as Roman Catholic.

Roman Catholic churches where my grandparents lived near Pittsburgh first had been established predominantly by Irish and Germans. When possible, late nineteenth-century Catholics settled parishes with immigrants from the same places who spoke the same languages. These national parishes fostered division and delayed Catholics' integration into American communities, which was a boon in some ways. American Protestants perfected many kinds of nasty anti-Catholicism, from lobbing incendiary words and deeds to harass immigrants, to lobbing actual incendiary devices at those strange people with their strong-smelling foods and strong drink and saints' days and loyalty to the pope.[13]

---

12. "Evangelicals and Catholics Together"; Fea, *Believe Me*; Williams, *Politics of the Cross*.

13. Dolan, *In Search of American Catholicism*, 71–126.

Be Not Afraid (Faith)

Once my grandparents moved to the Pittsburgh area, they centered their lives around St. Mark's, the Slovak church. Later they lived near the mostly German St. Mary's. The McKees Rocks of my mother's day boasted an ethnic church on just about every block, representing Slavs, Italians, and Germans, Roman Catholic and Eastern Orthodox believers. By the mid-twentieth century, upward and outward mobility of the children of immigrants thinned these congregations. They were reduced by the 1980s to clusters of older people in each cavernous old-world-style building, contending over which church was going to stay open and whose priest would say which Mass.[14]

My grandmother's social life revolved around St. Mary's, especially in her years as a widow. Baba invoked the Blessed Mother and policed the respect paid to God by our hemlines, necklines, and footwear, by the appropriate activities for Sunday (not laundry), and by the right ordering of festal meals. My mother grew up Catholic and did it well.

Between my mother's childhood and her coming of age, the Catholic Church changed. The Second Vatican Council happened when she was a young wife in the 1960s, having one baby after another. At that council, the visionary Pope John XXIII and the collected authority of cardinals and bishops gathered between 1962 and 1965 to bring the church up to date. How invigorating it must have been to be an American Catholic in the mid-1960s! In the rhetoric of the 1965 encyclical *Gaudium et spes* (*The Joy and the Hope*), Pope and Council fling wide the windows of the church and fling wide their arms to humanity, to poor suffering humanity wide-eyed and frightened like a fawn with buckling knees, and say, your problems are our problems! We care about you! Everything you worry about, you blustering humans terrified by your own clumsy electrified violence, we already have thought about those problems too! We can help you! God is the solution! It is a beautiful document.[15]

On top of all that was happening in Rome, 1960s America had a Catholic president. When I was growing up my mother had a print of Leonardo da Vinci's Last Supper above our kitchen table, which I thought was normal, even as I thought it was weird that some families kept portraits of the current pope next to one of John F. Kennedy alongside the Last Supper. My mother observed many rules of Catholic piety: no meat on Fridays in

---

14. McCartin, *Prayers of the Faithful*.
15. Pope Paul VI, *Gaudium et Spes*.

Lent, no saying "Oh my God," which was taking the Lord's name in vain. My siblings and I all were named after saints, most of them antique.

My mother lived a great range of Roman Catholic experience. She went on Des Colores retreats, led by Catholic charismatics to draw the churched into relationship with the Holy Spirit. When she retired to Florida, she put away the folk Mass and joined a choir that sang early modern hymns in complex four-part harmony. But in my childhood, she came into her own in the post-Vatican II church and it was her church that raised us. Ithaca Catholicism was politically active, had priests in slacks and nuns without habits, each called by their first names. We knew priests and nuns who had poured blood on missiles at nearby armories to protest wars in Latin America. We belonged to the Rochester diocese in upstate New York. If we had moved somewhere else or if my father had behaved better, we might have stayed in a more old-worldy church. But being welcomed by this strange place, our family as divorced strangers in it, meant being in the sort of church later called progressive. Religion felt relevant because it opposed war and exploitation and poverty as most people in Ithaca did. Smart people we knew, politically active people, generally were not atheists. The exception to the progressive trend was Immaculate Conception, a big older church downtown that my family rarely attended. I did not know what its name meant until I learned in graduate school that Pope Pius IX promulgated the dogma of the Immaculate Conception in 1854 as a way of doubling down on papal authority in a period of European secularization and nationalism. I had no idea, because the only other context I ever heard the word *immaculate* as a child was in reference to the homes of some of my mother's prayer-group ladies, which were very tidy. Our two primary parishes were St. Catherine of Siena, an A-frame with social-justice-minded folk, and the Cornell Catholic Community, which met in the auditorium of the neo-Gothic building attached to the law school, Anabel Taylor Hall, because Cornell was founded intentionally without a chapel or a religion department and these got jerry-rigged on later. Many different religious groups met in Anabel Taylor and the neo-Gothic grey stone itself seemed holy.

Sometimes my mother took us to home Mass, where a priest would celebrate the sacrament with a basket of torn bread in somebody's living room or, best, at one woman's lakeside cottage. Home Mass with Cayuga Lake rippling around made us feel like we practically were with Jesus at the Sea of Galilee. The kind woman with the lakeside cottage also took up

Be Not Afraid (Faith)

Clown Ministry. The inspiration for this 1970s mercy-work was the New Testament command to be fools for Christ. Clown ministers in face paint and balloon pants made me quail. Still, they were no weirder than many other things connected with Church in that period.

I was baptized as a baby. I made my First Communion with a white crown and veil and white stiff dress my sisters had worn before, standing up in front of the auditorium in Anabel Taylor Hall to receive the real body and blood of Jesus. In my Catholic childhood, we believed by doing. At dinner we folded our hands and said BlessUsOLord and crossed ourselves. I said the Our Father before bed and sometimes noted to God things I worried about or wanted to have happen. We went to Mass weekly. My mother sang songs loudly in church. She hated when musicians truncated the hymn before the last verse. When that happened and she knew the song, she sometimes kept standing in place while other people went out and she kept on singing.

After church we filed down to the One World Room for coffee hour. Somebody was always boycotting something, usually an agricultural commodity like table grapes or coffee, and some adult would report updates about that. In the multi-purpose gathering space in the basement of Anabel Taylor, under the watchful eyes of UN assemblies and migrant farm workers collaged on the wall, my siblings and I ate our way through a staggering number of donuts. My mother loved to talk to people after church, which left us unsupervised to eat so many donuts carefully cut into quarters, glazed and chocolate-frosted and cream-filled, and to scald our tongues on sludgy drinks made from dumping envelopes of cocoa powder into Styrofoam cups of hot water.

St. Augustine trembled on the edge of conversion a long time until he heard a voice saying, pick up and read. I read so many books when I was young and my mother said, why don't you read the Bible now and then too? I didn't. It was not because Catholics forbid Bible reading, as Protestants sometimes accuse. Before I went to college, the Bible was one of those books closed to me because it seemed boring, impenetrable, as though there was something about it which I already knew but also could not crack. I was convicted of my failure in high school when I read *Franny and Zooey* and learned the Jesus prayer and saw that the young genius Glass siblings were interested in spiritual texts as children. Growing up we had Bible story books for kids with bright simple illustrations, sans-serif font for guileless 1970s children. The longer-form Bible stories came in a hardcover book that overdid the rustic shepherd look for Jesus. At her bedside my mother had the Good News for Modern Man Bible with onion skin pages and occasional line drawings, stick-figure disciples around stick-figure Jesus at the Last Supper. There was a bookmark in it so I assumed she read it around bedtime.[16]

When we went to Mass on Sunday morning in the Anabel Taylor auditorium, we were never just mouthing words rotely, as Protestants sometimes accuse Catholics, or doing outward devotions with our hearts not in it. Hearing prayers and creeds in church made me know them not by rote but by ear, not by rote but by heart. I believe in God, the Father almighty, creator of heaven and earth, in Jesus Christ his son, begotten not made, and the Holy Spirit, the Lord the giver of life. I really did and I really do. I did not know exactly what I was saying, God from God, light from light, begotten not made. Not knowing didn't make saying it meaningless. I believed the creed to the extent I understood. I felt it was right and leaned that direction, the leaning and the creed itself responsible for the remainder. About the things of God there is a right somewhere, and I participated in it somewhat as I could and, since we all are wrong in part, well, we already know that.

I didn't know what it meant either to sing "Morning Has Broken" in God's direction, which we often did in church at Anabel Taylor. Though I didn't know exactly what a blackbird had to do with Jesus, the blackbird that spoke like the first bird, I thought it must be related to the Lord somehow, and I wanted the sunlight Eden saw play. When we sang songs like that in Anabel Taylor auditorium, I tried to screw forth sincerity to sing them with the same conviction involved in saying, Blessed is he who comes in the name of the Lord. Love the beauty of medieval cathedrals though I do, love my ancestors' backbreaking efforts to rebuild like cathedrals in heavy stones at St. Mary's or St. Mark's, I have never been able to recant the praise I learned at Anabel Taylor. There was a glimmer of divine presence in songs sung accompanied by guitar. Sometimes one of our first-name priests would play the guitar. I felt those stirrings, longings for the holy while sitting on red velveteen auditorium seats singing "Blowin' in the Wind" or "Kumbaya" or "I Am the Light," and passing the bread made the body of Christ hand to hand, from a wooden bowl with a whole-grain round pulled into shareable bits. I felt community with my fellow man despite the impossible awkwardness of holding the hand of the college student standing next to me with stringy hair and sweaty palms when we said the Our Father. I

---

16. St. Augustine, *Confessions*, 132–33.

Be Not Afraid (Faith)

felt something drawing me to God and I strained toward it, wanted it or at least wanted to want it and to be good. I was in a haze then anyway, my vision blurred by other thoughts and the fact that I always was carrying me around with myself wherever I went.[17]

But also, there was my aunt. My mother's youngest sibling belonged to a different generation, having hippie boyfriends, going to protests against the Vietnam war, dreaming of being an actress in New York. Not many years after my First Communion, Mother took us to visit her for Easter in Manhattan. As it grew near night that Saturday we were passing St. Patrick's Cathedral and my mother, guessing we might not go to church the next morning, said we should go in for some of the Easter Vigil service. At some point during the Mass my aunt started behaving strangely. She wasn't making a sound but had tears running down her face.

Something was up with her when we got back to her apartment. Somebody had thought ahead to buy egg dye as a way of keeping kids occupied. When we were coloring eggs, my aunt picked up a particularly vibrant green one and hurled it against the wall. She told us there was a demon in the egg and she cast him away. After that my mother sent us all to bed. They stayed up talking and my aunt described her experience in the cathedral as a conversion. The Lord Jesus appeared to me, she said, I got saved, grace poured all over me like melted butter. What do you mean you got saved, my mother demanded, you have been Catholic all your life. No, said my aunt, that was just going through the motions, I got saved, Jesus came to me in that cathedral and it was like an atomic bomb going off in my head.

Whatever had happened to my aunt, she thereafter seemed to want it to happen to us too. When she would call our house, everyone dreaded being the one to answer the phone. My aunt took seriously her duty to hold out for us the terms of salvation, presenting the facts, if you died tonight you might go to heaven or hell, you can be saved right now. Sometimes we had to handle the calls on our own. Usually my mother would be there to take the receiver and say, stop scaring my kids, my kids already know the Lord Jesus. I worried whether my aunt was right or my mother. I thought melted butter sounded okay but not the bomb in the head.

After my first semester of college, I was home on Christmas Eve when my aunt called. I had been feeling salvation anxiety. Advent should have

---

17. "Morning Has Broken," the Cat Stevens song adapted from Eleanor Farjeon's poem, and the folk song "Kumbaya," and Ray Repp's many songs, including "I Am the Light," regularly appeared in rotation at Cornell Catholic Community Mass.

that effect on people. Advent overlaps with American commercial shopping season and with cookie baking and merry making, but Catholics and others make December a period focused on the second coming of Jesus, not the first. The second will be judgment and fire. The way to prepare for it is with repentance and surrender, fear and trembling. At Mass on Christmas Eve the two comings can be brought together in great tenderness. That year I spent the service near tears, wondering how what the angels told the shepherds could be good news and wondering if I were saved or not. I thought everyone assembled in church on Christmas Eve, in satin dresses and snowy boots, was breathing a collective sigh of relief that Jesus didn't come back yet so they could still celebrate him as a baby. It was not at all clear to me that I was going to get saving, that the words of comfort delivered by Christmas would count for me. Grace taught my heart to fear and grace relieved it, as I learned from "Amazing Grace." When I answered the phone on Christmas Eve and my aunt told me to receive Jesus as my Lord and savior, it seemed plausible. That felt like an important moment, praying over the phone, and maybe it was, to save a wretch like me.

I became a wretched Protestant. I joined a college-student Christian fellowship when the semester started again. My new friends seemed convinced that Catholics were wrong in ways that had never occurred to me. When the other students in my fellowship group said that Catholics committed idolatry by worshiping saints or that Communion bread was not a piece of the flesh of Jesus, I came to agree. I thought I had to figure out the truth on all items of controversy, barely aware of how many times other people ran these same arguments in the last four hundred or so years. I grieved my family. Since my conversion depended not on believing in Jesus but believing in Jesus in this particular way, life-changingly different from the way I believed before, the new way had better be right. The problem was that my Protestant friends were good at naming what Catholics were wrong about but internally divided about what they thought was right.

I begged rides from my new friends to visit different churches to figure out which one was right. One week I went to the Lutheran service, which seemed a lot like Catholic Mass, as did the Episcopal service another week, though neither congregation seemed to want this resemblance pointed out. At the Mennonite church I was nervous the whole time about whether I was supposed to cover my head. The Methodists sang good hymns but did not have a clear stance on my doctrinal puzzles. For a while I went nondenominational with my fellowship group to a Bible church, whose name suggested old controversies simply could be ignored. After that, at a Presbyterian church at last I met some Protestants who acted like they knew they had things right. They were Calvinists, though they preferred to be called "Reformed," which seemed politer but also a dodge.

My new friends were largely uninterested in what were life-and-death questions for me, although they did agree one had to receive Jesus as Lord and Savior. Receiving Christ, asking Jesus to come into your heart, giving over your life to the Lord—these were synonyms for the one needful thing, according to my new friends. I had passed the test with my phone prayer. Receiving Christ seemed to me much harder than they let on. Confuting Catholics, my Evangelical friends emphasized salvation as gift, that there was no striving because God did everything for us. This contradicted my experience, because my fellowship friends also told me that now I had to give everything over to Christ and live my life for him. The next step, "sharing your faith," meant bringing others to Christ through presentation of a little booklet with four spiritual laws. I had never felt obligated to do much religious striving or proselytizing until I started hanging out with people who deplored striving. Asking Jesus in seems easy, but giving over your life or heart or self is much harder. I don't have an organ for that, an extra set of hands with which to hand myself over.

I liked the idea of receiving Christ because at base I think what Christians say about Jesus is true and is a big enough truth to absorb everything else. Still, self-abnegation is not only a discomfort but a contortion. My new habit of Bible reading introduced me to Ananias and Sapphira, a pair of new believers who pledged something to God but held back a portion for themselves so they were struck dead (Acts 5:1–11). I felt kin to them. At a Christian conference with my campus fellowship group, an older woman took me aside and advised that I just had to give up whatever I was holding back from the Lord. I told her what I was holding back was myself. She thought I was being mouthy or recalcitrant, as if covering up drug use or a bad boyfriend.

It has been useful to me to assume since then that nobody else quite knows either how to give themselves over to the Lord, to really and truly do it, not just go through motions. How *would* one do this? The Protestants who made most sense to me were the same ones who made the project of giving over oneself harder by getting rid of all the physical disciplines—vesture, gesture, and posture, kneeling and bowing and crossing oneself, fasting and prostrating oneself—through which the outer person accomplishes something on behalf of the inner person. I learned that some sixteenth-century Protestants were fond of the Prayer of Manasseh, where Manasseh says he repents by bending the knee of his heart. But how, Manasseh? The inner person wants to bow before God but can't really, since it is the outer person, the body, that bows. I would not know where to find the knees of my heart to bend them. If the inner person is what matters but the outer person cannot move it, then what does move the inner person? This problem went unacknowledged by my new fellowship friends, who sometimes, disconcertingly, asked Christ into their hearts more than once.

I did believe the good news, that Jesus came to save sinners of whom I am chief, and some days I felt it. Most days in practice I was a latter-day sixteenth-century zealot. All the things that Luther and Calvin and Zwingli and Andreas Bodenstein von Karlstadt and comrades objected to about Roman Catholicism rattled me too. When I was a child no one had justified to me the standard Catholic things, like purgatory, indulgences, the Blessed Virgin Mary, praying to saints, priestly corruption, riches lavished on buildings while the poor starved. So when Protestants railed at those things, I could not help but agree. The Catholics I asked to explain these bones of contention largely explained them away, as though it were all just a bunch of misunderstandings, Protestants protesting things that Catholics did not even actually believe. I made appointments to talk to priests. The first one was disappointingly evasive. He answered my urgent "how do I know if I'm saved" question with a request to define what "saved" meant to me, a fair question but not a very pastoral one. The next Cornell priest was hyper-Thomist, a favorite of the prayer-group ladies. In hindsight I appreciate how smart he was but at the time he seemed wily, smuggling unfamiliar interpretations of words like "freedom" and "happiness" into everyday language so at the end of homilies I felt tricked. Another priest spent our interview mostly expressing his regret that young adults these days disregard church teaching on contraception.

Is there a purgatory or not? Could I expect to go there, or ever get out, or what? I tried to shake the dust of Catholic misunderstandings off my feet. I could not quite explain why they were wrong but was sure it mattered whether they were. I felt that I was getting closer to God than when I was one of them. But one reason I could resonate with parachurch praise songs, the I-love-you-Jesus idiom of my new Evangelical friends, was that I had learned to feel that thing as a child on Sundays in the Cornell Catholic Community. The music played there in Mass that my mother kept

Be Not Afraid (Faith)

on cassette tape in car and kitchen, songs of love to God by Ray Repp and the Saint Louis Jesuits and the Monks of the Weston Priory, that music had imported into Catholicism yearnings like what I found later in Evangelical worship. If ever I felt like I had a relationship with God, it was this way. The Cornell Catholic Community prepared me to be a Protestant.

Rome beckoned now and then and occasionally I visited, sometimes literally. After college I went to Europe for the first time with my mother and brother. In Rome, we visited the church of St. Agnes, the beautiful Roman martyr who welcomed death rather than submit her body to violation, whose hair grew miraculously to shield her body from the lewd eyes of scoffers. I love Italy as people normally do. At the time, though, I mostly saw its saints and churches through Protestant eyes: so much stuff! so much heavy dark marble! so much lurid interest in the flesh, its lushness and torment!

Saints posed problems. Pressed on the question of praying to saints, conscientious Catholics will say, no, we aren't *worshiping* saints, we are venerating them. In the litany of saints, for instance—Saint Stephen, Pray for Us, Saint Vincent, Pray for Us, All You Holy Monks and Hermits, Pray for Us—congregations call on saints for intercession. But all my life I heard laypeople praying to saints. In Montepulciano we saw another St. Agnes, a thirteenth-century Tuscan Dominican who prayed so fervently she sometimes floated off the ground, and sometimes little cross-shaped flakes sweet and nourishing like manna fell from the sky around her. When St. Catherine of Siena went to visit the tomb of this St. Agnes and leaned down to kiss the feet of the uncorrupt body, one foot miraculously rose, a sign of Catherine's holiness and a kind of mutual blessing. Why does cross-shaped manna not fall from the sky when I pray? Why did St. Agnes not lift her foot when I visited?

I don't object to ranking some people holier than others. It seems just frankly true that some people are holier than others. But I wondered why my holiness was so unremarkable when I did so want to be close to God. I resisted believing holiness could be gotten by something I could do, like fasting or rosaries. Also I did not want to do those things. But, like other Protestants, I had objections that went beyond self-interest. The Protestant answers left open questions too, though. If all people are sinners in need of grace, why are some people better than others? If all true Christians receive Jesus, why aren't all equally aflame with love of Christ? I have been to Italy as often as I can manage since then. I find puzzles there: the lives of the saints, their spectacular self-denial, their mystical visions in mystical landscapes. Why would it seem right in the midst of the land of olive oil and honey to deny one's body and live on crickets? If something I could do could make me holier, I must be misunderstanding holiness.

Take up and read. The mysterious voice that drew St. Augustine into conversion spoke to me too. What I read in the New Testament I did not often find consoling. The pocket-sized New Testament that my fellowship group eagerly pressed into hands of seekers in dining hall or dorm lounge was full of hard sayings. My attention was drawn to those, presumably by the Holy Spirit. The words said things like, enter the narrow way for there are few that find it, or, the kingdom of heaven is harder to enter than a camel entering a needle's eye, or, many are called but few are chosen, or, the farmer plucks out the weeds and burns them in fire, or, seed sown on good soil bears fruit thirty or sixty or a hundred times but on poor soil, nothing. All sinners seemed not to be equal in the estimation of Jesus, but some people are likened goats not sheep, some are foolish bridesmaids not wise, some are lukewarm to be spewed out, and the unready will be cast into darkness with wailing and gnashing of teeth. What grace mostly taught my heart was to fear.

Somehow I overlooked the Puritans when I was in college. Somehow I came to them in the summer before I went to grad school. I took up a book called *The New England Mind: From Colony to Province* and read it. I did not really understand it but the people in it felt like companions, kneeling beside me with the knees of their heart. I sought them out that summer in other books because I found them saying things like, how may I know I am saved?, and, what if I am a gospel hypocrite?, and, if my name doesn't appear in the pages of the Bible, could that be evidence that I am going to hell? The Puritans refused not just the Hail Mary but the Our Father too. They objected to repeating rote prayers, because if you can't mean your words to God the first time then you should not be saying them. They agreed that God deserves all glory and right worship, and if they couldn't always get it up, they knew to mourn for their lumpish affections. They not only thought Catholics were wrong, as did my college fellowship group, they thought the pope was the antichrist. But unlike my fellowship group, they could say what was right about their answer to Catholic wrongs. From out of their midst they cast all the filthy remnants that more tepid Protestants retained, like the Church of England with its Book of Common Prayer. Critics accuse Puritans of hating Christmas. Not so. They had no particular gripe with

Be Not Afraid (Faith)

Christmas but also rejected Easter, the Book of Common Prayer, crosses and crossing oneself, kneeling, hymns, vestments, and church weddings, because God was not honored by human inventions. When I got to grad school I was walking across the quad with a group of new grad students, awkwardly posing as smart people, and my new advisor asked if anyone had ever read Perry Miller's *The New England Mind*. He asked me what I thought of the book's argument. I didn't think anything. I just thought the people in it made sense. I hoped they were wrong about salvation but they made sense.[18]

It was the enemies of Puritans who gave them that name. That word proved useful for long-term maligning. Puritans thought God saved only some and not all Christians. Conversion, to them, did not mean knowing Jesus saves but discerning whether you were among the group Jesus saved. Discerning grace might come after a period of deep sorrow for sin and repentance. There was no promise that any relief would follow repentance. Understandably it was a psychological strain to live this way. Under the revival preaching of his nephew Jonathan Edwards, in 1735 Joseph Hawley of Northampton, Massachusetts, slit his throat because he could not stand the Evangelical despair any longer, what it feels like when you know you deserve God's wrath and presume you will be getting it. Hawley would not have bent to kiss the toe of St. Agnes, but he knew that some people feel the love of God more than others, and that the problem was not whether you choose Christ but whether Christ chooses you.

I joined the Reformed grad students I knew at their Presbyterian church on Sundays, but not much happened there at Easter Vigil, so for that I went to the Catholic church on campus. I saw there not only my religious studies professor who taught the course on the Reformation, but more startling still, my advisor who studied Puritans, astonishing because I thought both of them should have known better. The cantor sang the Exsultet, the prayer that opens the Vigil Mass when the congregation stands around in the dark and the priest lights a fire and holds a towering Paschal candle marked with the wounds of Christ. The cantor sings that all time belongs to Christ, that God's love is boundless and merciful, O happy fault, O necessary sin of Adam, to gain for us so great a Redeemer.

The Vigil prayers poured grace on me almost like melted butter, and I felt grace through the next sunny day, Easter, feeling like there was nothing I had to do, nothing else that was expected of me, a rare feeling for

---

18. Miller, *New England Mind*.

a graduate student. Having seen my religious studies professor at Mass, I did make bold to visit him some weeks later to ask why anybody would continue to be Catholic once they knew about the Reformation. I tried to put it in historical terms: why would people in sixteenth-century Europe still attend Mass or their cousin's Catholic wedding once they heard they the real gospel, the message of the Reformers? Because they believed their eternal souls depended on the sacraments, he said, as though that were obvious, which I guess historically it was. He also pointed out that to scruple oneself away from a wedding or baptism or funeral was to tear apart family bonds and social ones. He was right. I had done that myself. Later when I took a class on St. Augustine from another religious studies professor who had converted to Catholicism, I asked him why he made the change and he told me conversion was first a matter of love, so I should not try to reason my way into it.

Love is more confusing than the good reasons one might become Reformed or Catholic. No sooner had I embraced Calvin and his followers and started attending a very Reformed Presbyterian church, than I discovered this church was patching passages from the Book of Common Prayer into its Sunday service. I loved those pieces until I discovered their source. I was so confused that I was ready to go back to being Catholic again, except that I was going to this Presbyterian church with the man I soon married, who, though no longer Baptist, was pretty well Protestant. Much later we became Anglican.

The year we got married we spent in Germany. In Europe then and later, I kept bumping into Catholic things that kept me Protestant. We visited Eastern Europe during Holy Week that year, with a stop to my mother's cousin in Slovakia. We made it to Litmanova late at night on Holy Thursday and went to sleep on a featherbed in the wooden house my cousin had built with his own hands. They served us a shot of vodka with our breakfast because we were special guests. Meanwhile a neighbor, back home after a few months in New Jersey, was summoned to help translate. While we nursed the vodka, she told us that there were apparitions in the town. We thought we had misunderstood her English. But this was no fault of her New Jersey translation. Since 1990, the Virgin Mary indeed had been appearing to girls in the town. Now many pilgrims were coming to the site. The next day we took a bus to Krakow. The church we tried to stop in for Easter Vigil was too packed to enter, crowds standing thick to the doors so we couldn't see anything, and the Mass was in Polish, so there was nothing to hear. I still thought then that worship required seeing and hearing. The next day, Easter, was sunny and I felt some of that unaccountable rest, that there was nothing more I had to do, though I was also sorry to be put out of the worshiping throng, because I had put myself out of it.

Evangelicals timid about sharing their faith are sometimes conceded the option of "lifestyle evangelism," a softer sell in which shy Christians wanting to tell others the good news just go about their life which, Jesus being what he is, will be so fruitful and radiant that passersby observing it will think, "I want what they have!" Then the Christian is supposed to tell them about Jesus. Sometimes I teach history classes in a study-abroad program in Italy, including field trips that bring mostly Protestant students to Catholic convents, meeting sisters mostly from the developing world ensconced in beautiful but depopulated old-world religious houses. Almost always the students will ask the sisters why they chose this life. Almost always a sister will say something like: "I never dreamed of this. I never planned for this, but I met God this way, I fell in love with God, God called me here, I am home." I want what they have.

While I was busy pitting Catholics and Calvinists against each other for the fate of my soul, other American Christians kept busy other ways. Some kept on loving justice and mercy and walking humbly with God. Some twisted fiery faith together with a few other strands like old nativism or new nationalism and put politics in place of creed as test of fidelity. Some found church itself nearly irrelevant, were spiritual but not religious, or were religious but de-institutionalized, or were flatly post-Christian. Some people who believed the gospel stopped. Some rejected Christianity or whatever was the religion of their youth but others, newly called Nones, with no affiliation or even necessarily rejection of religion, became pagan without the title. People once part of a Christian fold—pastors' kids, lapsed Christian musicians, academics raised in pious homes, exvangelicals—can find a creed in rejecting the old ones. Their stories go like this: now free of the cramped Christianity of well-meaning but ignorant parents, I once was found but now I'm lost, phew. These stories are mostly predictable and sometimes also tax charity.[19]

---

19. Williams, *Politics of the Cross*; McCammon, *Exvangelicals*.

WHAT'S STRANGE ABOUT THIS WAY OF EMBRACING CHRISTIANITY

What was strange to me when I thought I was becoming a Christian was that the old borders could be stepped over where they even were visible at all. The fact of divisions in the body of Christ is an ongoing sorrow and scandal. Though some Americans are active in their denominations, many Christians seem pretty much loose from those labels. American Christian experience could have gone so far to mending those divisions, to joining together as one body in the Lord. So much good could have come of American Christians' amnesia about things that seemed worth mutual murder a few centuries before. Sometimes American efforts in ecumenism can be tepid because sectarians see divisions not as tragedy but happy diversity of God's people.

Some of what is strange about American Christianity is strange in a good way, the way that made Tocqueville marvel. Many Americans might explain their choice of church by its social composition or neighborhood or children's ministries or service opportunities. Sects mostly do not dream of killing each other. Christians recognize each other as Christians. Evangelicals often are caring, careful people, contrary to the caricature casting them as sexist and racist, and often are ready to repent of injustice once it is pointed out.

The marketplace of religious ideas in America has manufactured products other than what Jesus has in mind. The megachurch, the body of Christ on earth as reimagined by car culture, made informality a high ideal, seeker-friendly aesthetics leaning away from churchy piety and toward an office-park shopping-mall vibe flowing with boutique-ish coffee, the last acceptable vice of the Jesus-loving, coffee as far from the donut-studded coffee hours of my childhood as east from west. These spaces are convenient and accessible, consecrated to fellowship. This sensibility taken further makes space itself obsolete to church, the body of Christ gathered virtually to watch a preacher on a screen. After COVID, some people may never go back to church in person.

As the last century turned to ours, American Christians might have felt confident, free to love God and their neighbors, post-Soviet Russia no longer needing our rosary intercession, American presidents appearing annually at the National Prayer Breakfast. However, many American Christians came to behave as embattled, confronting real and perceived threats to their faith: the shrinking, aging congregations; the visible presence of other believers in public squares, especially Muslim believers; popular and elite culture hostile or indifferent to religion and more aggressively secular. Evangelicals arrayed to win culture wars in the early twenty-first century found their own righteous camps riddled with scandal, scandals usually pertaining to money or sex. Catholics discovered a long and horrible history of covering up sexual abuse in the US and many other places around the world. Christians who were out of political ascendancy have gotten in again, a good number putting their support behind Donald Trump. Christians who are supposed to be known by their care for widow and orphan and stranger get more publicity for being otherwise.[20]

What's strange is that Americans kept being more religious even though Europeans declared that modernity was secular, but we may be getting into line with that version of modernity. What's strange is that American Christians do not actually have to take their cues from the marketplace in presenting religious ideas but often do. What's strange is that American Christians, given chance to love God and each other with old dividing walls of hostility levelled, build new walls. What's strange is that gestures mimicking excommunication are provoked here by moral questions rather than doctrinal ones, same-sex relationships or women preachers or mask wearing. What's strange is that many American Evangelicals, cut loose from dependence on the state, voluntarily pledge loyalty to politics and let themselves be led by strongmen making promises to retrofit America as Christian nation.

BETTER THINKING ABOUT BELIEVING OR HOW I STOPPED WORRYING AND LEARNED TO LOVE GOD

The religious communities my childhood met seemed to solve problems people perennially confront in practicing their faith. The future promised fellowship in spirit and truth, good works for the poor and oppressed, and free-world security and toleration. Instead many in the household of faith fell to fighting or fell away.

American conditions could make it so easy to follow God and serve him here and now. So many obstructions that might get in the way of worshiping God have been removed. Americans don't have to battle deadening rules of a state church. Americans don't face sword or ban. Americans now don't have to refight the Reformation every generation, and anyway, I

20. Smith, *American Evangelicalism*; Alberta, *Kingdom, the Power*.

already did that. We have keen awareness of our limits in getting answers right and should not fixate on internal divisions rather than troubles outside. Evangelical cooperation softens divisions among Protestants. Brothers and sisters in Christ can dwell in unity.

A lot of writing about how somebody learned to love God focuses too much on the writer when the focus should be God. St. Francis chose to show rather than tell, that right human response to the limits of how humans love God is tumbling around like a fool for Christ and falling face down crying with joy at the One who came to save us. Thomas Aquinas and Blaise Pascal both had mystical visions of God so flaming glorious that they laid aside their writings, all that like straw, said Thomas. Pascal said Fire, Fire, and named what he saw as not the God of the philosophers. I would prefer that the mystical vision complement, rather than blotting out, the kind of knowledge that reason offers. Are Pascal and Aquinas in heaven sitting around a table rubbing hands together in rueful glee that we fools still search for God by reading their books? It cannot possibly be the case that God's regard of me depends on my right opinion of God.

It is only more ridiculous to assume we can know that God doesn't exist. At the center of everything is not nothing or evil but God. God is not surprised and does not wear out; God gathers all together so that nothing is lost or wasted. The prophet Isaiah told Israel that God will never forget his people because he has carved them on the palm of his hand (Isaiah 49:15). At home when I was growing up, we did not have a portrait of the pope or JFK but we did have a little sculpture of this image, a carving of a child leaning its head into a large hand. A prayer-group lady gave it to my mother. I understood the sculpture's point.

I hope what I find is true might be useful to somebody else. Leading me to God is the fact that the very big and the very little both exist. The tiniest things are complex and intricate and have order, the cellular level, the atomic, the sub-atomic, and the particles below that, and at the very same time the universe is huge beyond human imagination such that humans must revert to measurements made of light. The world is good and it's good to be alive in it, even as the pain and decay of the earth burrow down deep enough to need a special measure beyond human calculation, whatever is the opposite of light years. These sets of things are both true at once too, the fact of the good and the incidence of the bad. Think how much grief is stored in the happy fault. The only way I make sense of the world's mourning and weeping is by the scales of the good that overwhelms them.

Be Not Afraid (Faith)

    The self-denying contortions of the saints, lovely as some of them are, express fidelity beyond my reach that I am not sure God has intended or desires. Jesus, the Word who became flesh, spoke relief over human life and showed that embodiment is good. This is the first coming and the second coming of Christ put back together. Suffering may be unavoidable in this vale of tears and God may use it for good, but I don't warm to it. Saints Agnes, pray for us. Saint Thomas Aquinas and Saint Blaise Pascal, Saint Joseph Hawley, pray for us. What a relief, that there is not nothing in the universe and God loves what God has made. What people make of that can make a difference in the span of the life they receive.

Bibliography

Adams, Sarah LaChance, and Caroline R. Lundquist, eds. *Coming to Life: Philosophies of Pregnancy, Childbirth, and Mothering*. New York: Fordham University Press, 2012.

Adamy, Janet. "Why Americans Are Having Fewer Babies." *Wall Street Journal*, May 26, 2023. https://www.wsj.com/articles/why-americans-are-having-fewer-babies-3be7f6a9.

Alberta, Tim. *The Kingdom, the Power, and the Glory: American Evangelicals in an Age of Extremism*. New York: Harper, 2023.

Alon, Titan, Matthias Doepke, Jane Olmstead-Rumsey, and Michèle Tertilt. "The Impact of Covid-19 on Gender Equality." NBER Working Paper 26947, National Bureau of Economic Research, April 2020. https://www.nber.org/system/files/working_papers/w26947/w26947.

Andersen, Lydia, and Zachary Scherer. "US Marriage and Divorce Rates Declined in Last Ten Years." US Census Bureau, December 7, 2020. https://www.census.gov/library/stories/2020/12/united-states-marriage-and-divorce-rates-declined-last-10-years.html.

Apple, Rima D. *Perfect Motherhood: Science and Childrearing in America*. New Brunswick, NJ: Rutgers University Press, 2006.

Augustine, Saint. *Confessions*. Translated and edited by Henry Chadwick. Oxford New World Classics. Oxford: Oxford University Press, 1991.

Axtell, James. *The School upon a Hill: Education and Society in Colonial New England*. New York: Norton, 1976.

Banks, Jennifer. *Natality: Toward a Philosophy of Birth*. New York: Norton, 2023.

Bailey, Beth L. *From Front Porch to Back Seat: Courtship in Twentieth-Century America*. Baltimore: Johns Hopkins University Press, 1988.

Baum, Devorah. *On Marriage*. New Haven: Yale University Press, 2023

Bayne, Brandon. *Missions Begin with Blood: Suffering and Salvation in the Borderlands of New Spain*. New York: Fordham University Press, 2021.

Berg, Anastasia, and Rachel Wiseman. *What Are Children For? On Ambivalence and Choice*. New York: St. Martin's, 2024.

Bernard, Jesse. *The Future of Marriage*. New York: World, 1972.

Beste, Jennifer. *College Hookup Culture and Christian Ethics: The Lives and Longings of Emerging Adults*. Oxford: Oxford University Press, 2017.

Beston, Paul. "When High Schools Shaped America's Destiny." *City Journal*, September 2017. https://www.city-journal.org/article/when-high-schools-shaped-americas-destiny.

Bibliography

Bitar, Adrienne Rose. *Diet and the Disease of Civilization*. New Brunswick, NJ: Rutgers University Press, 2018.

Bittman, Mark. *Animal, Vegetable, Junk: A History of Food, from Sustainable to Suicidal*. New York: HarperCollins, 2021.

Boushey, Heather. *Finding Time: The Economics of Work-Life Conflict*. Cambridge: Harvard University Press, 2016.

Bowles, Nellie. "The Sperm Kings Have a Problem: Too Much Demand." *New York Times*, January 28, 2021/updated June 25, 2023. https://www.nytimes.com/2021/01/08/business/sperm-donors-facebook-groups.html.

Bracken, Peg. *The I Hate to Cook Book*. New York: Harcourt, Brace & World, 1960.

Brake, Elizabeth, ed. *After Marriage: Rethinking Marital Relationships*. Oxford: Oxford University Press, 2016.

Buechner, Frederick. *Wishful Thinking; A Seeker's ABC*. New York: HarperCollins, 1993.

Callard, Agnes. "Acceptance Parenting." *The Point*, October 2, 2020. https://thepointmag.com/examined-life/acceptance-parenting/.

Carnes, Natalie. *Motherhood: A Confession*. Redwood City, CA: Stanford University Press, 2020.

Carney, Timothy, P. *Family Unfriendly: How Our Culture Made Raising Kids Much Harder Than It Needs to Be*. New York: HarperCollins, 2024.

Caton, Donald. *What a Blessing She Had Chloroform: The Medical and Social Responses to the Pain of Childbirth from 1800 to the Present*. New Haven: Yale University Press, 1999.

Celello, Kristin. *Making Marriage Work: A History of Marriage and Divorce in the Twentieth-Century United States*. Chapel Hill: University of North Carolina Press, 2009.

Chan, Jessamine. *The School for Good Mothers*. New York: 37Ink, 2022.

Cherlin, Andrew J. *The Marriage-Go-Round: The State of Marriage and Family in America Today*. New York: Knopf, 2010.

Clinton, Hillary Rodham. *It Takes a Village, and Other Lessons Children Teach Us*. New York: Simon & Schuster, 1996.

Coffman, Elesha. *Turning Points in American Church History: How Pivotal Events Shaped a Nation and a Faith*. Grand Rapids: Baker Academic, 2024.

Coontz, Stephanie. "How to Make Your Marriage Gayer." *New York Times*, February 13, 2020. https://www.nytimes.com/2020/02/13/opinion/sunday/marriage-housework-gender-happiness.html.

———. *Marriage, A History: From Obedience to Intimacy or How Love Conquered Marriage*. New York: Viking, 2005.

Cott, Nancy F. *Public Vows: A History of Marriage and the Nation*. Cambridge: Harvard University Press, 2000.

Crebs, Albin. "Family and Career." *New York Times*, January 3, 1972. https://www.nytimes.com/1972/01/03/archives/family-and-career.html.

Crittenden, Ann. *The Price of Motherhood: Why the Most Important Job in the World is Still the Least Valued*. 10th Anniversary ed. New York: Picador, 2010.

Crocker, Betty. *Betty Crocker's New Picture Cookbook*. New York: McGraw Hill, 1961.

Cusk, Rachel. *A Life's Work*. New York: Picador, 2001.

Dabling, Brandon. *A New Birth of Marriage: Love, Politics, and the Vision of the Founders*. Notre Dame: University of Notre Dame Press, 2022.

BIBLIOGRAPHY

De la Cruz, Sor Juana Inés. *Selected Writings: Poems, Protest, and a Dream.* Translated by Margaret Sayers Peden. New York: Penguin, 1997.

De Marneffe, Daphne. *Maternal Desire: On Children, Love, and the Inner Life.* New York: Little, Brown & Company, 2004.

Declercq, Eugene, and Laurie Zephyrin. "Maternal Mortality in the United States: A Primer." *Commonwealth Fund Data Brief,* December 2020. https://www.commonwealthfund.org/sites/default/files/2020-12/Declercq_maternal_mortality_primer_db.pdf.

Delbanco, Andrew. *College: What It Was, Is, and Should Be.* Princeton: Princeton University Press, 2012.

Dolan, Jay P. *In Search of an American Catholicism: A History of Religion and Culture in Tension.* Oxford: Oxford University Press, 2002.

———. *The American Catholic Experience: A History from Colonial Times to the Present* New York: Doubleday, 1985.

Douthat, Ross. *Bad Religion: How We Became a Nation of Heretics.* New York: Free Press, 2012.

Dreier, Hannah "Kids on the Night Shift." *New York Times Magazine,* September 20, 2023. https://www.nytimes.com/2023/09/18/magazine/child-labor-dangerous-jobs.html.

Druckerman, Pamela. *Bringing up Bébé: One American Mother Discovers the Wisdom of French Parenting.* New York: Penguin, 2012.

Dubofsky, Melvyn, and Joseph A. McCartin. *Labor in America, A History.* 10th ed. New York: Wiley-Blackwell, 2024.

Dunak, Karen. *As Long as We Both Shall Love. The White Wedding in Postwar America.* New York: New York University Press, 2013.

Eisenberg, Arlene, Heidi E. Murkoff, and Sandee E. Hathaway. *What to Expect When You're Expecting.* New York: Workman, 1984.

Eisenmann, Linda. *Higher Education for Women in Postwar America, 1945–1965.* Baltimore: Johns Hopkins University Press, 2006.

Elkins, Kathleen Gallagher. *Mary, Mother of Martyrs: How Motherhood Became Self-Sacrifice in Early Christianity.* Eugene, OR: Wipf & Stock, 2018.

Emba, Christine. *Rethinking Sex: A Provocation.* New York: Sentinel, 2017.

Epstein, Randi Hutter. *Get Me Out: A History of Childbirth from the Garden of Eden to the Sperm Bank.* New York: Norton, 2010.

Eskridge, William N., Jr., and Christopher R. Riano. *Marriage Equality: From Outlaws to In-Laws.* New Haven: Yale University Press, 2020.

"Evangelicals and Catholics Together: The Christian Mission in the Third Millennium." *First Things,* May 1994. https://www.firstthings.com/article/1994/05/evangelicals-catholics-together-the-christian-mission-in-the-third-millennium.

Fea, John. *Believe Me: The Evangelical Road to Donald Trump.* Grand Rapids: Eerdmans, 2018.

———. *Was America Founded as a Christian Nation? A Historical Introduction.* Louisville Westminster John Knox, 2011.

Feeney, Matt. *Little Platoons: A Defense of Family Life in a Competitive Age.* New York: Basic, 2021.

Fields, Robin. "What to Know about the Roiling Debate over U.S. Maternal Mortality Rates." *ProPublica,* April 5, 2024. propublica.org/article/what-to-know-maternal-mortality-rates-debate.

Bibliography

Finkel, Eli. *The All-or-Nothing Marriage: How the Best Marriages Work.* New York: Dutton, 2017.

Finn, S. Margot. *Discriminating Taste: How Class Anxiety Created the American Food Revolution.* New Brunswick, NJ: Rutgers University Press, 2017.

Fissell, Mary E. "Hairy Women and Naked Truths: Gender and the Politics of Knowledge in 'Aristotle's Masterpiece.'" *William and Mary Quarterly* 60 (2003) 43–74.

Friedan, Betty. *The Feminine Mystique.* Introduction by Anna Quindlen. New York: Norton, 2001.

Fukuyama, Francis. *The End of History and the Last Man.* New York: Free, 1992.

———. *The Great Disruption: Human Nature and the Reconstitution of the Social Order.* New York: Free, 2000.

George, Paul S. "The Early Success of Middle School Education." *Middle School Journal* 41:1 (September 2009) 4–9.

Gershon, Ilana. "'I'm Not a Businessman, I'm a Business, Man': Typing the Neoliberal Self into a Branded Existence." *HAU: Journal of Ethnographic Theory* 6:3 (2016) 223–46.

Gessen, Keith. *Raising Raffi: The First Five Years.* New York: Penguin Random House, 2022.

Gilman, Charlotte Perkins. *Women and Economics.* Boston: Small, Maynard & Company, 1898.

Goldin, Claudia. *Career and Family: Women's Century-Long Journey Toward Equity* Cambridge: Harvard University Press, 2022.

———. "How America Graduated from High School: 1910 to 1960." NBER No. 4762, Working Paper. Department of Economics, Harvard University, 1994. https://dash.harvard.edu/bitstream/handle/1/32785054/w4762.pdf?sequence=1.

Hartog, Hendrik. *Man and Wife in America: A History.* Cambridge: Harvard University Press, 2002.

Harvey, Paul. *Through the Storm, Through the Night: A History of African American Christianity.* Lanham, MD: Rowman & Littlefield, 2011.

Hatch, Nathan O. *The Democratization of American Christianity.* New Haven: Yale University Press, 1989.

Hayden, Dolores. *The Grand Domestic Revolution: A History of Feminist Designs for American Homes, Neighborhoods, and Cities.* Cambridge: MIT Press, 1981.

Hays, Sharon. *The Cultural Contradictions of Motherhood.* New Haven: Yale University Press, 1998.

Hazard, Leah. *Womb: The Inside Story of Where We All Began.* London: Ecco, 2023.

HHS Fact Sheet. "In Vitro Fertilization (IVF) Use Across the US." US Department of Health and Human Services, March 13, 2024. https://www.hhs.gov/about/news/2024/03/13/fact-sheet-in-vitro-fertilization-ivf-use-across-united-states.html.

Hochschild, Arlie, and Anne Machung. *The Second Shift: Working Families and the Revolution at Home.* Rev. ed. New York: Penguin, 2012.

Horn, Claire. "Ectogenesis Is for Feminists." *Catalyst: Feminism, Theory, Technoscience* 6:1 (2020). https://doi.org/10.28968/cftt.v6i1.33065.

Horowitz, Julie Menace, Nikki Graf, and Gretchen Livingston. "Marriage and Cohabitation Rates in the US." Pew Research Center, November 6, 2019. https://www.pewresearch.org/social-trends/2019/11/06/marriage-and-cohabitation-in-the-u-s/.

Howard, Agnes R. *Showing: What Pregnancy Tells Us about Being Human.* Grand Rapids: Eerdmans, 2020.

———. "Changing Expectation: Prenatal Care and the Creation of Healthy Pregnancy." *Journal of the History of Medicine and Allied Sciences* 75:3 (2020) 324–43.

Bibliography

Howard, Thomas Albert. *God and the Atlantic: America, Europe, and the Religious Divide.* Oxford: Oxford University Press, 2011.

Hoyert, Donna L. "Maternal Mortality Rates in the United States." CDC National Center for Health Statistics E-Stats, May 2024. https://www.cdc.gov/nchs/data/hestat/maternal-mortality/2022/maternal-mortality-rates-2022.pdf.

Hunnicutt, Benjamin Kline. *Free Time: The Forgotten American Dream.* Philadelphia: Temple University Press, 2013.

Inhorn, Marcia C. *Motherhood on Ice: The Mating Gap and Why Women Freeze Their Eggs.* New York: New York University Press, 2023.

Innes, Stephen. *Creating the Commonwealth: The Economic Culture of Puritan New England.* New York: Norton, 1995.

Jefferson, Thomas. *Notes on the State of Virginia* (1785). Electronic ed. Documenting the American South, 2006. https://docsouth.unc.edu/southlit/jefferson/jefferson.html.

Jellison, Katherine. *It's Our Day: America's Love Affair with the White Wedding, 1945–2005.* Lawrence: University Press of Kansas, 2008.

Jewison, Norman, dir. *Fiddler on the Roof.* Culver City, CA: United Artists, 1971.

Jones, Lucy. *Matrescence: On the Metamorphosis of Pregnancy, Birth, and Motherhood.* New York: Penguin, 2023.

Juravich, Tom. *At the Altar of the Bottom Line: The Degradation of Work in the 21st Century* Boston: University of Massachusetts Press, 2009.

Kamp, David. *The United States of Arugula: The Sun Dried, Cold Pressed, Dark Roasted, Extra Virgin Story of the American Food Revolution.* New York: Crown, 2009.

Kass, Amy A., and Leon R. Kass, eds. *Wing to Wing, Oar to Oar: Readings on Courting and Marrying.* Notre Dame: University of Notre Dame Press, 2000.

Kauffman, Jonathan, and Bon Appetit Staff. "How 1971 Changed the Way We Eat Forever." *Bon Appetit,* May 23, 2021. https://www.bonappetit.com/gallery/1971-changed-food-forever.

Kearney, Melissa S. *The Two-Parent Privilege: How Americans Stopped Getting Married and Started Falling Behind.* Chicago: University of Chicago Press, 2023.

Kerber, Linda K. *Women of the Republic: Intellect and Ideology in Revolutionary America.* Chapel Hill: Omohundro Institute of Early American History and Culture and University of North Carolina Press, 1980.

Kessler-Harris, Alice. *Out to Work: A History of Wage-Earning Women in the United States.* 20th anniversary ed. New York: Oxford University Press, 2003.

———. *Women Have Always Worked: A Concise History.* Urbana: University of Illinois Press, 2018.

Kittay, Eva Feder. *Love's Labor: Essays on Women, Equality, and Dependency.* 2nd ed. New York: Routledge, 2019.

Kliff, Sarah. "Most Rural Hospitals Have Closed Their Maternity Wards, Study Finds." *New York Times,* December 4, 2024. https://www.nytimes.com/2024/12/04/health/maternity-wards-closing.html.

Kline, Wendy. *Coming Home: How Midwives Changed Birth.* Oxford: Oxford University Press, 2019.

Koven, Seth, and Sonya Michel. *Mothers of a New World: Maternalist Politics and the Origins of Welfare States.* New York: Routledge, 1993.

Krueger, Alyson. "First Comes Marriage. Then Comes the Rehearsal Dinner." *New York Times,* September 12, 2024/updated October 6, 2024. https://www.nytimes.com/2024/09/12/style/rehearsal-dinner-after-wedding.html.

Bibliography

Labaree, David F. *The Making of an American High School: The Credentials Market & the Central High School of Philadelphia, 1838–1939.* New Haven: Yale University Press 1992.

La Berge, Ann F. "How the Ideology of Low Fat Conquered America." *Journal of the History of Medicine and Allied Sciences* 63:2 (April 2008) 139–77.

Lareau, Annette. *Unequal Childhoods: Class, Race, and Family Life.* 2nd ed. Berkeley: University of California Press, 2011.

Lemann, Nicholas. *The Big Test: The Secret History of the American Meritocracy.* New York: Farrar, Strauss, and Giroux, 1999.

Lewis, Sophie. *Full Surrogacy Now: Feminism Against Family.* New York: Verso, 2019.

———. "Surrogacy as Feminism: The Philanthrocapitalist Framing of Contract Pregnancy." *Frontiers: A Journal of Women's Studies* 40:1 (2019) 1–38.

Lichtenstein, Nelson. *State of the Union: A Century of American Labor.* Princeton: Princeton University Press, 2002.

Malesic, Jonathan. "'Nothing Is to Be Preferred to the Work of God': Cultivating Monastic Detachment for a Postindustrial Work Ethic." *Journal of the Society of Christian Ethics* 35:1 (2015) 45–61.

Manning, Wendy D., Susan L. Brown, Krista K. Payne. "Two Decades of Stability and Change in Age at First-Union Formation." *Journal of Marriage and Family* 76:2 (2014) 247–60. https://www.ncbi.nlm.nih.gov/pmc/articles/PMC4136537/.

Marche, Stephen. *The Unmade Bed: The Messy Truth about Men and Women in the 21st Century.* New York: Simon & Schuster, 2017.

Mazzoni, Cristina. *Maternal Impressions: Pregnancy and Childbirth in Literature and Theory.* Ithaca, NY: Cornell University Press, 2002.

———. *The Women in God's Kitchen: Cooking, Eating, and Spiritual Writing.* New York: Continuum, 2005.

McCammon, Sarah. *The Exvangelicals: Loving, Living, and Leaving the White Evangelical Church.* New York: MacMillan, 2024.

McCartin, James P. *Prayers of the Faithful: The Shifting Spiritual Life of American Catholics.* Cambridge: Harvard University Press, 2010.

McMillen, Sally G. *Lucy Stone, An Unapologetic Life.* Oxford: Oxford University Press, 2015.

Mead, Rebecca. *One Perfect Day: The Selling of the American Wedding.* New York: Penguin, 2007.

Meilaender, Gilbert C. *Bioethics: A Primer for Christians.* 4th ed. Grand Rapids: Eerdmans, 2020.

———. "The New Fatherhood." *First Things*, February 1, 2003. https://www.firstthings.com/article/2003/02/the-new-fatherhood.

Meilaender, Gilbert C., ed. *Working: Its Meaning and Its Limits.* Notre Dame: University of Notre Dame Press, 2000.

Mendelson, Cheryl. *Vows: The Modern Genius of an Ancient Rite.* New York: Simon & Schuster, 2024.

Miller, Perry. *The New England Mind: From Colony to Province.* Cambridge: Harvard University Press, 1953.

Mintz, Steven. *The Prime of Life: A History of Modern Adulthood.* Cambridge: Harvard University Press, 2015.

Molnar, Szilvia. *The Nursery.* New York: Pantheon, 2023.

Morgan, Marabel. *The Total Woman.* Old Tappan, NJ: Revell, 1973.

Bibliography

Moss, Michael. *Hooked: Food, Free Will, and How the Food Giants Exploit Our Addictions.* New York: Random House, 2022.

Mudry, Jessica J. *Measured Meals: Nutrition in America.* Albany: State University of New York Press, 2009.

Mundy, Liza. *Everything Conceivable: How the Science of Assisted Reproduction is Changing Our World.* Rev. ed. New York: Anchor, 2008.

Neem, Johann. *Democracy's Schools: The Rise of Public Education in America.* Baltimore: Johns Hopkins University Press, 2017.

Nestle, Marion. *Food Politics: How the Food Industry Influences Nutrition and Health.* Berkeley: University of California Press, 2013.

Noll, Mark A. *The Civil War as a Theological Crisis.* Chapel Hill: University of North Carolina Press, 2015.

Noll, Mark A., David W. Bebbington, and George M. Marsden, eds., *Evangelicals: Who They Have Been, Are Now, and Could Be.* Grand Rapids: Eerdmans, 2109.

Noll, Mark A., David Komline, and Han-Luen Kantzer Komline. *Turning Points: Decisive Moments in the History of Christianity.* 4th ed. Grand Rapids: Baker Academic, 2022.

Norris, Kathleen. *The Quotidian Mysteries: Laundry, Liturgy, and "Women's Work."* New York: Paulist, 1998.

O'Connell, Meaghan. *And Now We Have Everything: On Motherhood Before I Was Ready.* New York: Little, Brown, and Company, 2018.

O'Toole, James M. *The Faithful: A History of Catholics in America.* Cambridge: Belknap, 2008.

Parker-Pope, Tara. "Masks, No Kissing, and 'A Little Kinky': Dating and Sex in a Pandemic." *New York Times*, June 11, 2020. https://www.nytimes.com/2020/06/11/well/live/coronavirus-sex-dating-masks.html.

Paul VI, Pope. *Gaudium et Spes, Pastoral Constitution on the Church in the Modern World Promulgated December 7, 1965.* https://www.vatican.va/archive/hist_councils/ii_vatican_council/documents/vat-ii_const_19651207_gaudium-et-spes_en.html.

Pieper, Josef. *Leisure the Basis of Culture.* Edited by James V. Schall. San Francisco: Ignatius, 2009.

Pinsker, Joe. "'Intensive' Parenting is Now the Norm in America." *The Atlantic*, January 16, 2019. https://www.theatlantic.com/family/archive/2019/01/intensive-helicopter-parenting-inequality/580528/.

Plant, Rebecca Jo. *Mom: The Transformation of Motherhood in Modern America.* Chicago: University of Chicago Press, 2010.

Pollan, Michael. *Food Rules: An Eater's Manual.* New York: Penguin, 2009.

———. *The Omnivore's Dilemma.* New York: Penguin, 2007.

The President's Council on Bioethics. "Human Cloning and Human Dignity: An Ethical Inquiry." July 2002. https://www.theatlantic.com/family/archive/2019/01/intensive-helicopter-parenting-inequality/580528/.

Reiner, Rob, dir. *When Harry Met Sally.* Beverly Hills, CA Castle Rock, 1989.

Rich, Adrienne. *Of Woman Born: Motherhood as Experience and Institution.* New York: Norton, 1976.

Richardson, Sarah S. *The Maternal Imprint: The Contested Science of Maternal-Fetal Effects.* Chicago: University of Chicago Press, 2021.

Rothman, Barbara Katz. *A Bun in the Oven: How the Food and Birth Movements Resist Industrialization.* New York: New York University Press, 2016.

Rowbotham, Sheila. *Dreamers of a New Day: Women Who Invented the Twentieth Century.* New York: Verso, 2011.

Bibliography

Rumer, Masha. *Parenting with an Accent: How Immigrants Honor Their Heritage, Navigate Setbacks, and Chart New Paths for Their Children*. Boston: Beacon, 2021.

Sandberg, Sheryl. *Lean In: Women, Work, and the Will to Lead*. New York: Knopf, 2013.

Sargeant, Leah Libresco. *The Dignity of Dependence: A Feminist Manifesto*. Notre Dame: University of Notre Dame Press, 2025.

Senior, Jennifer. *All Joy and No Fun: The Paradox of Modern Parenthood*. New York: Ecco, 2014.

Shapiro, Laura. *Perfection Salad: Women and Cooking at the Turn of the Century*. Reprinted with a new Introduction. Berkeley: University of California Press, 2009.

———. *Something from the Oven: Reinventing Dinner in the 1950s*. New York: Penguin, 2005.

Silbergeld, Ellen K. *Chickenizing Farms and Food: How Industrial Meat Production Endangers Workers, Animals, and Consumers*. Baltimore: Johns Hopkins University Press, 2016.

Simpson, Kathleen Rice. "Trends in Labor Induction in the United States, 1989 to 2020." *MCN: The American Journal of Maternal/Child Nursing* 47:4 (2022) 235.

Skenazy, Lenore. *Free-Range Kids: How to Raise Safe, Self-Reliant Children (Without Going Nuts with Worry)*. New York: Wiley & Sons, 2009.

Skocpol, Theda. *Protecting Soldiers and Mothers: The Political Origins of Social Policy in the United States*. Cambridge: Belknap, 1995.

Slater, Dan. *Love in the Time of Algorithms: What Technology Does to Meeting and Mating*. New York: Current, 2013.

Slaughter, Anne-Marie. "Why Women Still Can't Have It All." *The Atlantic*, August 15, 2012. https://www.theatlantic.com/magazine/archive/2012/07/why-women-still-cant-have-it-all/309020/.

Smajdor, Anna, and Ruth Deech. *From IVF to Immortality: Controversy in the Era of Reproductive Technology*. Oxford: Oxford University Press, 2007.

Smith, Christian. *American Evangelicalism Embattled and Thriving*. Chicago: University of Chicago Press, 1998.

Spar, Debora L. *The Baby Business: How Money, Science, and Politics Drive the Commerce of Conception*. Cambridge: Harvard Business Review Press, 2006.

Stephenson, Joan. "Rate of First-time Cesarean Deliveries on the Rise in the US." *JAMA Health Forum* 3:7, July 12, 2022. https://jamanetwork.com/journals/jama-health-forum/fullarticle/2794350#google_vignette.

Strasser, Susan. *Never Done: A History of American Housework*. New York: Henry Holt, 1982.

Syfers, Judy. "I Want a Wife." 1970. Reprinted at https://www.columbia.edu/~sss31/rainbow/wife.html.

Thelin, John R. *Going to College in the Sixties*. Baltimore: Johns Hopkins University Press, 2018.

———. *A History of American Higher Education*. 3rd ed. Baltimore: Johns Hopkins University Press, 2019.

Thomas, Marlo, et al. *Free to Be . . . You and Me*. New York: Bell Records, 1972.

Thistle, Susan. *From Marriage to the Market: The Transformation of Women's Lives and Work*. Berkeley: University of California Press, 2006.

Tocqueville, Alexis de. *Democracy in America*. Translated by Gerald Bevan. Introduction by Isaac Kramnick. New York: Penguin, 2003; Online text at https://www.marxists.org/reference/archive/de-tocqueville/democracy-america/ch18.htm.

Bibliography

Traister, Rebecca. *All the Single Ladies: Unmarried Women and the Rise of an Independent Nation*. New York: Simon & Schuster, 2016.

Turpin, Andrea L. *A New Moral Vision: Gender, Religion, and the Changing Purposes of American Higher Education, 1837–1917*. Ithaca, NY: Cornell University Press, 2016.

Ulrich, Laurel Thatcher. *Goodwives: Image and Reality in the Lives of Women in Northern New England, 1650–1750*. New York: Knopf, 1980.

———. *A Midwife's Tale: The Life of Martha Ballard, Based on Her Diary, 1785–1812*. New York: Knopf, 1990.

Van der Lugt, Mara. *Begetting: What Does It Mean to Create a Child?* Princeton: Princeton University Press, 2024.

Vandenberg-Daves, Jodi. *Modern Motherhood: An American History*. New Brunswick, NJ: Rutgers University Press, 2014.

Veit, Helen Zoe. *Modern Food, Moral Food: Self-Control, Science, and the Rise of Modern American Eating in the Early Twentieth Century*. Chapel Hill: University of North Carolina Press, 2013

Wallace, Carol McD. *All Dressed in White: The Irresistible Rise of the American Wedding*. New York: Penguin, 2004.

Walzer, Judith. *Brought to Bed: Childbearing in America, 1750–1950*. New York: Oxford University Press, 1988.

Warner, Judith. *Perfect Madness: Motherhood in the Age of Anxiety*. New York: Riverhead, 2005.

Wertz, Richard W., and Dorothy C. Wertz. *Lying-In: A History of Childbirth in America*. New Haven: Yale University Press, 1989.

The White House–National Economic Council, Clinton Archives. "Raising Student Achievement." https://clintonwhitehouse4.archives.gov/WH/EOP/nec/html/doc062100.html.

Wilcox, Brad. *Get Married: Why Americans Must Defy the Elites, Forge Strong Families, and Save Civilization*. New York: Broadside, 2024.

———. "Soulmate Marriage, RIP." Institute for Family Studies, March 30, 2020. https://ifstudies.org/blog/soulmate-marriage-rip.

Wilder, Laura Ingalls. *Farmer Boy*. Harper Collins Classics Imprint. New York: Harper Collins, 2008.

Williams, Daniel K. *The Politics of the Cross: A Christian Alternative to Partisanship*. Grand Rapids: Eerdmans, 2021.

Winship, Michael P. *Godly Republicanism: Puritans, Pilgrims, and a City on a Hill*. Cambridge: Harvard University Press, 2012.

Witte, John. *From Sacrament to Contract: Marriage, Religion, and Law in the Western Tradition*. Louisville: Westminster John Knox, 1997

Wolf, Jacqueline H. *Deliver Me from Pain: Anesthesia and Birth in America*. Baltimore: Johns Hopkins University Press, 2009.

Yenor, Scott. *Family Politics: The Idea of Marriage in Modern Political Thought*. Waco, TX: Baylor University Press, 2011.

Zelizer, Viviana A. *Pricing the Priceless Child: The Changing Social Value of Children*. Princeton: Princeton University Press, 1994.

www.ingramcontent.com/pod-product-compliance
Lightning Source LLC
Chambersburg PA
CBHW030858170426
43193CB00009BA/657